CHRYSANTHEMUM GROWING

D0315255

ALADDIN
JAPANESE, INCURVED

CHRYSANTHEMUM GROWING

by

W. E. SHEWELL-COOPER

M.B.E., N.D.H., F.L.S., F.R.S.A., DIP.HORT. (WYE)

Principal of The Horticultural Training Centre
Director of The Horticultural Educational and Advisory Bureau
Late Command Horticultural Officer, Eastern and S.E. Commands
Previously Horticultural Superintendent, Swanley Horticultural College
and sometime Horticultural Adviser, Warwickshire and Cheshire County Councils

THE GARDEN BOOK CLUB

121 *Charing Cross Road, London, WC* 2

Made and printed in England by
STAPLES PRINTERS LIMITED
at their Rochester, Kent, establishment

CONTENTS

ACKNOWLEDGEMENTS

The Publishers would like to express their thanks to Messrs. H. Woolman Ltd. for permission to use the photographs facing pages 64, 112, 128 and 144; to Messrs. Keith Luxford Ltd. for the use of the frontispiece and the photographs facing pages 16 and 44; and to Messrs. Sutton & Sons Ltd. for the use of the illustrations on pages 152 and 153.

ILLUSTRATIONS

PREFACE

IT is curious the way things happen. Messrs W. H. Smith have an excellent magazine, and one day a well-known contributor of theirs had an article in it about selling books and mentioned that among gardening books there was nothing like a good book on chrysanthemums from the sales point of view. This led to my friend Mr Bernard Whatley (we had served together in the war) writing to me on behalf of Messrs Allan Wingate about this very book.

I had often toyed about writing on chrysanthemums and yet the idea had never crystallised somehow. Bernard Whatley's letter did the trick. Here it is!

I suppose I can date back my interest in chrysanthemums to 1925 when I became Horticultural Superintendent at the Cheshire School of Agriculture. My right-hand man in the garden, Bert Shaw, was a real expert in growing them and I learnt a great deal from him. Year after year we tried out new varieties together and reported on them in the horticultural press. We grew them indoors and under glass. We tried covering with lights in the open and preventing the early frosts from damaging them by using candles in between the rows. In fact, I got the chrysanthemum 'fever' very badly indeed. That 'fever' has lasted until this day.

When I became Superintendent at the Swanley Horticultural College I went on growing chrysanthemums, and when I left to become Principal of the Horticultural Educational and Advisory Bureau, which was then at Hextable, the chrysanthemum culture continued with the help of Mrs Gwenneth Johnson, then Miss G. Wood, Dip.Hort. (Swanley).

Stuart Ogg, who is perhaps better known as the 'Dahlia King', is also an excellent chrysanthemum grower, and it was a pleasure to be able to go up and see what he was doing near Swanley at any time. His nursery was only a mile from my home. We were all indeed delighted when he named that very fine October-flowering chrysanthemum Irene Shewell-Cooper after my wife. It is a glorious shade of deep amber on very strong stems, and it is no wonder that it got a First-Class Certificate from the National Chrysanthemum Society.

I never write a book without receiving help from many friends. John B. Stevenson, for instance, one of the leading commercial chrysanthemum growers, has given me permission to quote fairly extensively from his excellent book *Chrysanthemum Stopping Illustrated*. He has also lent me a number of photographs. Others I should like to thank are Mr Frank Shepherd, my present head gardener, and Miss Mary Morris, A.R.H.S., one of our Horticultural lecturers, who have both read through the proofs and made suggestions.

Finally, a thank-you to Miss Margaret Foley for typing the whole of the script so patiently.

W. E. SHEWELL-COOPER

Principal.

The Horticultural Training Centre, Thaxted, Essex.

CHAPTER I

The Background of the Chrysanthemum

THERE is probably no flower that enjoys a greater world-wide popularity than the chrysanthemum. I have met it all over Europe. It is grown with great success in Australia and South Africa. It is very much admired and made a fuss of in the United States and is grown to perfection in Holland, Denmark and Belgium. It is estimated that in Great Britain some 7,000 acres were devoted to the culture of this flower alone in 1939, and it may be that this acreage has been passed in 1951. The value of chrysanthemums grown under glass is probably in the region of £500,000 a year at the time of writing.

As to history, it is known that the chrysanthemum was cultivated successfully in China in 500 B.C., and there is little doubt that as long ago as A.D. 900 actual chrysanthemum shows were held in Japan. It is undoubtedly an Eastern flower, and thousands of years ago was venerated by the Chinese and almost worshipped. It is recorded that in the eighteenth century the first chrysanthemums were brought to Western Europe. Records show that it was the captain of a French ship who brought specimens to his home country in 1789. It was not long before plants started coming over to Great Britain regularly, and it is known that by 1795 a number of varieties were growing in this country and they were described in books written by experts at that time.

It is interesting to record that by 1820 a dozen different kinds were being cultivated in Great Britain and that in 1826 over fifty varieties were known and grown. We have to thank Robert Fortune for bringing many new chrysanthemum types from China and Japan in his journeys, and our thanks must also go to a vast number of European gardeners for hybridising and thus raising many new varieties from seed. It was thus that the novelties started to be introduced.

One never knows, of course, what is going to happen with regard to chrysanthemums, and many were intrigued when in 1945 they first saw the various colours in the Favourites, which bloomed from early December till early January. It is useful to have a selection of chrysanthemums which will provide colour through the two bleakest months of the year.

The great thing fifty years or so ago was to produce huge blooms like mops, but today the majority of gardeners are far more interested in flowers with a good strength of stem and firmness of foliage, and so in most shows today five blooms are exhibited in a vase rather than the old-fashioned one huge bloom method. Why, in the days of long ago, the huge specimen blooms had to be exhibited on boards! They were too cumbersome to go in a vase. The popularity of this Queen of Autumn flowers has never decreased. The dahlia has tried its best to take first place, and so latterly has the Michaelmas daisy, but again and again the chrysanthemum has held its own as the best cut-flower of them all. It lasts well, and provides plenty of colour in the autumn and winter months; there is a warmth about the blooms that somehow cheers up the duller season of the year, and taking it all round, it is not a plant that is too difficult for the beginner to try to grow.

There are, of course, singles and doubles. There are Cascades and baby Charms. There are Pompons and anemone-flowered types, and all these unusual kinds are featured in Chapter XV. Yes, with the chrysanthemum you have the kind of plant that suits everyone. The writer is, however, a little 'unhappy' with the way that commercial growers have been doing everything possible to bring the chrysanthemum season on earlier and earlier, for to buy this flower in July, as is quite possible today, seems to him to be extending the season too far and is tending to make the housewife tired of buying chrysanthemums by the time it comes to Christmas and the New Year.

One reason, perhaps, why the chrysanthemum is so popular is because it is so hardy. It is true that in very frosty seasons, early in October most plants are damaged, but it is not unusual (and sometimes to the commercial grower's regret) to find chrysanthemums in full bloom up to Christmas out of doors, even as far north as Birmingham, while in parts of Hampshire and Somerset Korean varieties may, in mild winters, go on flowering until the end of January. Statistics seem to show that we in this country will have to rely on our own efforts (a good thing!) for very many years to come, because chrysanthemum flowers and stems are rather heavy and bulky, and for this reason we are never likely to get very big import consignments from abroad.

The chrysanthemum may come from the East, but it has been naturalised in this country for so many years now that it is undoubtedly British, and more British perhaps than any other flower. We have to thank the National Chrysanthemum Society for the tremendous amount of work done since the founding of that august body as long ago as 1846 at Stoke Newington. No specialist society has done more to foster the growth of any plant along sensible lines than the N.C.S., and any interested in the growing of this flower should certainly become a member.

CHAPTER II

Classifying Chrysanthemums Officially

IT is as well to know the official classification of chrysanthemums as laid down by the National Chrysanthemum Society and agreed to by the R.H.S. I have purposely, therefore, included the necessary information in this chapter and have given a number of examples in each case.

INDOOR VARIETIES

Section I. Exhibition Incurved
  (*a*) Large-flowered.
     Examples: Annie Curry, Ondine, Monument.
  (*b*) Medium-flowered.
     Examples: Coronation Gold, Penrod, Progress.

Section II. Large Exhibition
     Examples: Edna Green, Majestic, H. E. Trueman.

Section III. Large Exhibition Incurving
     Examples: Candeur, Comrade, Graham Luxford, Linella.

Section IV. Medium Exhibition
     Examples: Elegance, Leonard Shoesmith, Mona Davis.

Section V. Reflexed Decoratives
     Examples: Edith Alston, Enton Beauty, Loveliness.

Section VI. Incurving Decoratives
     Examples: Coralie, Constance Baker, Southern Beauty.

Section VII. Anemones

(a) Large-flowered, i.e. with a diameter of five inches and upwards.
Examples: Admiration, Captivation, Citrus Queen.

(b) Medium-flowered, i.e. with a diameter of three inches but normally less than five inches.
Examples: Ceres, Elspeth, Heloïse.

(c) Small-flowered, i.e. Anemone Pompons, with a diameter of two inches and less than three inches.
Examples: Calliope, Mr Astie.

Section VIII. Pompons

(a) Large-flowered, i.e. with a diameter of two inches and upwards.
Examples: Mdlle Élise Dordan, Dresden China.

(b) Small-flowered, i.e. with a diameter of less than two inches.
Examples: Baby, Ethel, Hilda Canning.

Section IX. Singles

Varieties with not more than five rows of ray florets.

(a) Large-flowered, i.e. with a diameter of five inches and upwards.
Examples: Broadacre, Cleone, Peter Robinson.

(b) Medium-flowered, i.e. with a diameter of three inches but normally less than five inches.
Examples: Golden Seal, Mason's Bronze, Orange Glory.

(c) Small-flowered, i.e. with a diameter of less than three inches.
Examples: Godfrey's Gem, Market Gem.

Section X. Spidery, Plumed and Feathery

Examples: King of the Plumes, Mrs Carter, Mrs Filkins.

Section XI. Any Other Types
> *Examples:* Madam Brinquier, Rayonnante.

OCTOBER-FLOWERING VARIETIES

Section XVI. Reflexed
- (*a*) Large-flowered.
  > *Examples:* Cranfordia, Mrs T. Riley, Treasure.
- (*b*) Medium-flowered.
  > *Examples:* Commando, Yellow Gown.

Section XVII. Incurving
- (*a*) Large-flowered.
  > *Examples:* Dorothy Wilson, Forward.
- (*b*) Medium-flowered.

OUTDOOR VARIETIES

Definition of an Early-flowering Chrysanthemum: An early-flowering chrysanthemum is a variety which blooms in a normal season in the open ground before 1st October without any protection whatsoever. This definition does not debar exhibitors from protecting blooms from weather damage.

Section XX. Incurved
- (*a*) Large-flowered.
  > *Examples:* Empire White, George McLeod, Shirley Cream.
- (*b*) Medium-flowered.
  > *Examples:* Arctic Circle, Harvest Moon, Mrs Irene Torrance.
- (*c*) Small-flowered.
  > *Example:* Moonstone.

Section XXI. Reflexed
- (*a*) Large-flowered.
  > *Examples:* Barbara, Hope Valley, Imperial Yellow.

KEITH LUXFORD

Facing page 16

(*b*) Medium-flowered.
  Examples: Hurricane, Ruby, Sweetheart.
(*c*) Small-flowered.
  Examples: Firedrake, Sparkler, Wendy.

Section XXII. Incurving
  (*a*) Large-flowered.
    Examples: Bronze McLeod, E. Crossley, Una.
  (*b*) Medium-flowered.
    Examples: Migoli, Wharfedale Yellow.
  (*c*) Small-flowered.
    Example: Ivory.

Section XXIII. Singles
  (*a*) Large-flowered.
    Examples: Daphne, Major Robertson, Sandy Lawson.
  (*b*) Medium-flowered.
    Examples: Bessie, Caradoc, Nectar.

Section XXIV. Pompons
  (*a*) Tall.
    Examples: Cream Bouquet, Mosquito.
  (*b*) Dwarf.
    Examples: Anastasia, Tiny-Tot.

Section XXV. Any other types (including Koreans and Charms)

B

CHAPTER III

The Meaning of the Words

IT has been customary with a number of gardening books to have a kind of glossary at the end, and when a reader comes across a word or a term he does not understand, this glossary is dutifully turned up and the explanation discovered. This seems somehow the wrong way to go about it, and therefore as there are a very large number of words used in the jargon of the chrysanthemum-grower, we are starting right away with this dictionary, which it is hoped will enable any beginner to read the book with intelligent interest.

Stool

It will be as well to start with the plant as it is in the autumn or winter, after the blooms have been cut, for then you have left the root part of the plant and above it a fairly thick stem, which by then will be quite hard and may be only 6 inches long. This 'clump' together with its short old stem is known as the stool.

Sucker

Having dug up the stool and taken off some of the soil and brought it into the greenhouse (see Chapter IV), growths will start to develop from the roots of the stool, and these are known as suckers. These suckers which are usually rooted may be detached from the stools and be dibbled out in boxes or frames.

Cuttings

From the sides of the stem of the stools or from the base

there will develop growths which are removed in January or February and are dibbled out into boxes (see Chapter V).

Striking cuttings

A cutting (whether a basal cutting or a stem cutting) is said to have struck when it throws out its own roots. When it is first pricked out into a box the leaves flag because the base of the cutting has no method of getting hold of water to make up for the transpiration which is taking place. The leaves 'sweat', as it were, and having done this, they call upon the stem for more moisture, and because there are no roots below, the stem cannot oblige. When a cutting has struck, however, the leaves 'perk up' because the roots are starting to do their work.

Compost

This is a confusing term, because it is sometimes used to indicate the rotting down of vegetable refuse or straw for producing an excellent substitute for farmyard manure; and it is equally well employed for describing the soil mixture that is needed for striking the cuttings in boxes or growing the chrysanthemums on in pots. Again and again this book will refer to the John Innes Composts, sometimes called the J.I. Composts, and full details and instructions on the making of these special soil mixtures or composts needed for chrysanthemums will be found in Chapter VI.

Node

This means a joint in a stem. It is the part of the stem that normally bears a leaf, or leaves. There is usually a little swelling at that point. The area of stem in between two nodes is known as the inter-node.

Axil of leaf

Actually the axil of a leaf is the angle between the upper

side of the leaf and the stem. In the axil of a leaf may be found buds or little laterals.

Fillis

A kind of string which is used by gardeners for tying up plants. You can have two-ply fillis, three-ply fillis, and even four-ply fillis.

Hardening off

When plants have been growing in a greenhouse and so have been nice and warm, it is a mistake to put them straight out from this temperature into the cold ground and into a spot where they will have to put up with the normal outside weather. Therefore a gardener takes the plants out of the greenhouse and puts them into a frame or under cloches, where there is some protection but a good deal more air. Gradually he removes the glass protection in the day time until the plants are hard and can go out into the open.

pH

Scientists have agreed to express the degree of acidity of soil by what seems a queer notation, i.e. pH_7. This represents the neutral point; figures less than 7 indicate the degree of acidity, and figures more than 7 show the degree of alkalinity. It will thus be seen that a soil which is pH_4 is far more acid than a soil that is pH_6.

Basal growths

Another name for suckers. It is usual to remove these completely when the stools are brought into the house for the production of cuttings.

Stock plants

Another name for the stools. It usually refers to special plants which are retained, as the chrysanthemum grower says, for stock, that is to say for the production of cuttings. During the summer he may take the trouble to mark certain plants which are specially good, specially floriferous, or specially healthy, with a label, and these plants when cut down he describes as his stock plants. As a result, he says, 'I shall have a better stock next year'.

Natural break

When a plant is allowed to grow naturally it produces what is known as a 'break bud'. This is a small flower bud which grows at the tip of the main stem and as the result of its production the plant is checked and a number of branches are produced. Therefore, to allow a plant to break naturally, as it is called, means that you allow it to produce its branches when it will, without adopting any artificial method of inducing side growths to develop.

Timing, pinching or stopping

These three terms are used by gardeners to indicate that they are pinching out the growing point of a plant in order to cause the shoots in the axils of the leaves to grow out. They do this before the break bud develops naturally, and they do it in order to ensure that branches develop much earlier. The word 'timing' was introduced because when pinching off the growing point of a young plant you can make it flower earlier, or make it flower, so to speak, before its natural time. This is important for commercial growers, who like to get their blooms in early for market. It is important for those who exhibit and want to have the flowers ready for a certain show, and it is equally important for northerners, for instance, who want to produce blooms outside before there is a bad frost.

Crown buds

Having allowed a plant to break naturally, or having

stopped it, three, four or even five branches may be produced. Now each one of these will eventually produce a
flower bud at the terminal end, and these are known as
first crown buds. If there were four branches, there would
be four first crown buds.

Now if the gardener cares to pinch off the growing points
of these branches he carries out an operation known as 'the
second stopping', with the result that from, say, the four
branches (see illustration, page 61) eight branches are produced, and at the tip of each of these flower buds will develop,
and these in their turn are known as second crown buds.
Thus our four original branches now have eight sub-branches,
so to speak, and of course eight second crown buds.

Securing the bud

Now if you understood, with the help of the drawings,
what has been said above, it is necessary to go one step
further. When the bud does make its appearance at the end
of each shoot, then if you want a good-sized bloom you
make absolutely sure or, so to speak, you make it secure,
by pinching off all the little shoots and unwanted little
flower buds which are to be found in the axils of the leaves.
In this way, only one flower bud is left to develop at the
tip of each branch. Some people call this operation 'taking
the bud', but most gardeners use the term 'securing the
bud'.

Spray chrysanthemums

During the securing of the bud the operation known as
'disbudding' is carried out. The result is that you only get
a few big blooms; one, in fact, on the end of each branch.
If, on the other hand, no disbudding is carried out, then a
very much larger number of small flowers are produced and
the flowers, instead of being described as disbudded blooms,

are described as 'spray'. Commercial growers say, for instance, that they cannot sell 'spray stuff' in years when there is plenty of good disbudded bloom about. A plant grown 'spray' is one therefore that is allowed to grow naturally and to develop all its flower buds.

Sports

Sometimes a chrysanthemum plant will produce one branch or lateral bearing a different coloured flower. The variety may be normally a pink, and all of a sudden the gardener finds one branch bearing a bronze flower. The plant is then described as having sported, and what is virtually a new variety, i.e. the pink form, is called a 'sport'. It is said that this tendency to sport results from the fact that many of the newer varieties are products of crossing one colour with another. In the cells of the plant one colour may predominate but another colour may be present, and then this different colour appears as quite distinct from the true shade of the plant. Sometimes, not only does sporting occur from the coloration point of view, but the shape of the blooms may quite change, and also vigour and time of flowering.

The shoots produced in the axils of the leaves of a 'sporting' branch may be struck as described in Chapter V, and thus the new variety is perpetuated.

Scientifically it is said that the bud sports are due to a re-arrangement of the chromosomes in the plant cells.

Terminal bud

The term 'a terminal bud' is used to describe a flowering bud at the apex of a growth. This is quite different from a crown bud, where growths will start and develop beyond it. Commercial growers usually complain that the flowers from such buds are rather small. They are certainly compact.

A gardener who does not want a plant to bloom on the crown buds removes them and the growths which develop from below produce terminal buds.

Standing ground

When chrysanthemums are grown in pots it is necessary to stand these in the open during the summer and then bring them into the greenhouse about the end of September – sometimes a little earlier in the north, and maybe a little later in the south.

In order to prevent the roots of the chrysanthemum growing out of the pots into the ground on which they are standing, and to prevent worms from working their way up into the pots through the drainage hole, the soil is covered with coal ashes to a depth of 3 or 4 inches. Generally speaking, there is a fair amount of drainage underneath and in addition there are posts and wires to which the bamboos which are supporting the chrysanthemums can be tied, and this prevents the pots blowing over.

Ray floret and disc floret

In the single chrysanthemums the florets are of two kinds. There are disc florets in the centre, forming what is normally called the eye, and ray florets around the outside, which most amateurs just call 'petals'. Ray florets are, of course, really little flowers on their own. They contain the stigma, rather like two prongs of a fork, and it is on to this that the pollen lands. It then fertilises the ovary, which is at the base of the ray floret, and a seed or seeds are produced.

In the disc floret there are stamens which produce the pollen, and this is normally carried by insect visitors to the stigmas. Generally speaking, the stamens do not ripen simultaneously with the stigma in the same floret, and so self-fertilisation is very unlikely indeed. Very occasionally the forked stigmas bend back so far that they actually touch the pollen grains, and then of course self-fertilisation does take place.

Seedlings

New varieties are described as 'seedlings' when they have actually been raised from seed by specialists who transfer the pollen from one variety to the stigmas of another by hand. They remove any disc florets there are first, so as to make certain that no self-pollination can take place. Their problem often is that it is very difficult to get male pollen from double varieties, because this is only produced by the disc floret, and in a double variety disc florets may be absent or there may be very few of them.

Anticipated natural break

If the gardener is dealing with a variety that produces an abundance of shoots early on, he usually pinches out the tip of the plant before the break bud is seen, and thus anticipates what is going to happen naturally. Hence, the term used above. As a result, flowers will be produced which are called the first 'crown' buds.

Counting down

When the growths have developed after a natural break or an anticipated natural break, and there are more than are needed to produce a good crop of large flowers, the surplus ones are removed. This is known commercially as 'counting down'. This work may be done either at the first stop or after the second stop, and in the latter case the plant flowers on the second crown buds.

Third crowns

Very occasionally late varieties are stopped three times with the idea of trying to produce a very late crop of flowers, say, for the Christmas trade. These third-crown flowers are seldom first class, but to the trade grower they are often very valuable.

CHAPTER IV

Taking Care of the Stools

AS propagation normally takes place by means of cuttings, it is necessary to take the utmost care of the stools on which these cuttings are produced. It is for this reason that a special chapter is devoted to the subject.

There are one or two old-fashioned varieties of chrysanthemums, like the Masses or Goachers, which are usually propagated by taking off the suckers or side growths in the autumn and wintering these in frames. This is the exception rather than the rule, especially today. Another method which some amateurs adopt is to risk leaving the stools in the ground throughout the winter and then to dig them up in the spring and divide them, planting out the divided portions in well-manured land. Either of these methods can be adopted by those who have no frames or greenhouse. The suckers from the stools could be over-wintered in this case under continuous cloches.

As the stools are to be, in fact, the stock plants, it is extremely important to make certain that the varieties are true to name and type and that they are absolutely healthy during the summer. It always pays to mark the best plants when they are flowering, either with a label or a coloured bamboo, and thus only to save the marked stools in the autumn for propagation purposes. Stick to the best specimens each year and you will build up a better strain of the variety concerned. Far too many poor chrysanthemums are grown each season because the gardener does not take care to choose only the best stools for propagation purposes.

Remember that each stool should produce about five

good cuttings. Estimate, therefore, how many plants will be needed in the spring, and save the number of stools accordingly. There are two methods of ensuring excellent cuttings: The first is to take the stools into the greenhouse before they are cut down. This makes it possible for the leaves of the plants to pass back every bit of manufactured plant food to the roots before the leaves die naturally. Only when the leaves have died are the stems cut down to within, say, 6 inches of ground level. This will be done three weeks to a month after the plants have been taken in under cover. This method is very seldom adopted because the plants take up so much room in the greenhouse and few people can spare the space or the time for this special refinement.

Normally, then, the old stems are cut down to within 4 to 6 inches of ground level, and any leaves that appear below this point are removed to prevent decay. It is important not to leave the stools in the ground too long after the blooms have been cut. It is not so much that frost will harm the old plants, but the wet conditions of winter certainly do not improve them. In fact, those who *have* to keep the chrysanthemum stools in the flower border during the winter usually take the precaution of surrounding them with a 2½-inch layer of very coarse sand or well-weathered coal ashes, the idea being to keep the area around each stool dry, as well as to prevent damage by slugs and snails. Covering individual stools with large lantern cloches is another method of giving good protection.

In the north, where stools will be killed through being left in the open, a plan many amateurs adopt is to dig them up and to pack the stools tightly in boxes with plenty of horticultural peat put in between. They are then kept absolutely dry in a frost-proof shed, a loft or a garage, or even a spare room, and then when it comes to March the boxes are sprinkled with a little tepid water which, of course, is

soaked up by the peat and as a result the stools are stimu-
lated and cuttings start to be produced as a result. A mixture
of equal parts of horticultural peat, sharp silver sand and
really good soil can then be applied around the stools so as
to encourage cuttings to be produced in sufficient numbers.

Warm-water treatment

One of the worst pests of chrysanthemums is undoubtedly
the eelworm (see page 173). This first of all causes the lower
leaves of the plants to die, and then the trouble gradually
extends upwards. The plants are generally poor, the upper
leaves will hang down and appear mottled and sometimes
will have brown triangular patches; the flower buds may be
weak, and if the terminal buds are destroyed poor lateral
shoots develop with small malformed smooth-edged leaves.

Plants that have been attacked by eelworm in the summer
even ever so slightly (and in most gardens today there does
seem to be some eelworm infection) must be given what is
called warm-water treatment. The old growth is cut down
to within 4 inches of soil level and the stools should then
be shaken to remove all loose earth. After this, it helps if
the roots can be put under a tap of running water to wash
the remaining soil away. The stools to be treated are then
put in warm water at a temperature of 110 deg. F. for thirty
minutes. After this they should be taken out and be cooled
off in cold water before they are either boxed up or planted
into sterilised soil in frames. The production of cuttings is
usually delayed by two or three weeks when this method is
adopted, but it does ensure that eelworm-free plants are
produced.

Latterly, gardeners who have not wished to wait for the
half-hour period have found it possible to treat the stools
at a higher temperature, viz. 115 deg. F. for five minutes
only if they are small stools and fifteen minutes if they are

large. Whichever method is adopted, care must be taken to
see that the temperature of the water never reaches more
than 1 or 2 degrees higher than the figure given, nor should
the period be longer. If stools are 'overdone', there is a
likelihood of them being killed. Sometimes after this treatment, varieties are shy in producing cuttings. In this case
the plan should be to leave an extra long length of stem so
as to allow stem cuttings to develop. Varieties that are slow
to produce basal cuttings will often make up for it in their
stem cuttings.

Hygiene

It does help if all leaves are removed, not only from the
plants but from the soil surface as well, just before the stools
are lifted. Any suckers that appear at that time can be cut
off also, and all this material should be burned. The eelworm
is such an insidious pest that it never pays to allow some of
the leaves, or even pieces of the leaves, to fall to the ground
because the minute transparent eelworms roll themselves up
like a watch spring inside portions of dead foliage and can
withstand death for three years or more in the soil in this
condition. The moment the right moisture conditions occur
afterwards they can become active once more and 'swim'
up the moisture film on the outside of the chrysanthemum
stems and so get into the leaves.

Bulk treatment

Those who are growing very large numbers of chrysanthemums will want to get their stools lifted by the end of
October, before the serious winter rains. The plants will be
brought into a cold greenhouse after all the soil has been
shaken off and the basal growths have been removed. The
stools will be packed together as close as possible in beds
about 4 feet wide on the soil of the greenhouse. Then before

covering the stools with an inch layer of deacidified horticultural sedge peat or, better still, with the John Innes Potting
Compost No. 1, it is convenient to spray them with a nicotine wash as a precaution against aphides (or green fly)
(formula $\frac{3}{4}$ ounce of nicotine, 4 ounces of Shellestol to
10 gallons of water). The covering material should be
watered lightly from time to time to help to encourage
cutting production, care being taken never to produce
sodden conditions. The atmosphere should be buoyant, so
ensure that there is adequate ventilation.

The stools will be packed tightly together in groups of
a variety, and a space of 1 foot should be left between the
stools of one variety and another. See that the batches are
labelled clearly, and as the cuttings are taken it is quite
a good plan to place them into seed trays labelled with the
name of the variety so that there can be no doubt, when
the cuttings arrive at the potting shed, as to their name.

The stools of pot plants

As the pot plants are grown in the greenhouse in the
winter months and some varieties may not flower until
January, it is not possible to cut them down by the end of
October as in the case of the early-flowering varieties. It is
possible, however, to mark the best plants with labels or
little lengths of coloured worsted and then to cut down the
branches to within 6 inches of pot soil level the moment
flowering is over. At the same time, all the sucker growths
will be trimmed just below soil level and all the old leaves
will be removed for burning.

The pots will be watered but of course never over-
watered, with the result that cuttings will be produced from
the stools or cut-down stems which may be struck in early
January in the case of the December varieties, and early in
February in the case of the January varieties. As there is

often trouble with aphides at this period of the year it does pay to syringe the plants with nicotine from time to time, as advised on page 31.

The time factor

Gardeners sometimes want to know how long it takes for suitable growths to be reproduced from a stool to take as cuttings. The answer is that if the stools are of December-flowering varieties, and are placed into the propagating house at a temperature of, say, 40 to 45 deg. F., as described on page 30, a number of shoots $2\frac{1}{2}$ to 3 inches long should have been produced well above the level of the peat or John Innes Potting Compost by the middle of February.

With the early-flowering varieties brought into the house in November it should be possible to take cuttings at the end of December or early in January, with the result that in many kinds flowers may be expected early in August. If the gardener fails to take the cuttings until early in February, because he did not bring the stools in under cover until early December, then he might delay the flowering of a particular variety until late in August. It does therefore pay to get the stools in under cover sufficiently early if the gardener's aim is to produce early blooms.

Boxing versus soil 'blocks'

Many gardeners find it convenient to knock the stools out of the pots and then to tap the balls or blocks of soil on to a fork handle or even the side of the pot and so remove the bulk of earth from the roots. The stools are then packed tightly into fairly deep boxes, like potato chitting trays, where they are covered with the John Innes Potting Compost or horticultural peat. Being in wooden trays in this way the stools are easy to handle, and furthermore there is little difficulty in keeping one variety per box.

TAKING CARE OF THE STOOLS   33

Where there are no boxes and it is desired to wash the pots or at least to stand them out in the open where they can be cleaned by the rain and the elements, the plan is just to knock the ball of soil or block of soil out of the pots and then to stand these in serried rows in the greenhouse, where they take up less room than when they were in pots. These balls of soil are watered from time to time, they are also syringed over to keep the atmosphere humid, and nicotine is used as a spray to keep down aphides.

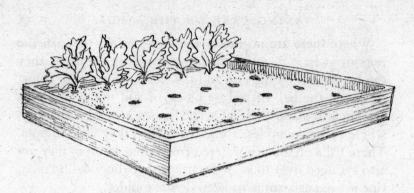

Fig. 1. *Cutting box with cuttings inserted. Note spacing.*

CHAPTER V

Plant Raising by Cuttings

UNDOUBTEDLY the easiest and best way of producing new plants is by means of cuttings, and in fact, in the previous chapter, we have been concentrating on the care of the stools because it is these, as has been explained, which are to produce the young growths suitable to take as cuttings. These cuttings should not be too fleshy. Most beginners imagine that you should go for the strong thick shoot, whereas the more wiry growth invariably makes the best cutting, roots quicker than the fleshy one, and makes a better plant in the end (see photograph, page 36).

It is important to have the stools in a house where the glass is absolutely clean, because you always get better wiry shoots that way. Soft fleshy growths never make good plants in the long run. Not only must the glass be clear, but there must be no pests and diseases in the early stages. Reference has already been made to green fly, but in addition thrips and the leaf-miner maggot can be very troublesome in the shoot and cutting stages. The regular spraying with nicotine does give effective control, especially if a good spreader such as Shellestol is added. Under hygienic conditions, with plenty of air and plenty of light, good growths should be produced which will root easily.

Cuttings

The young growths which appear from the base of a stool are severed from the stool and trimmed to form what is known as 'cuttings'. Some varieties are shy at sending basal shoots and therefore one is forced to take cuttings from the side of the stool itself – these are known as 'stem cuttings'. Friendly Rival and American Beauty are both varieties of this kind. Cuttings should, however, always be taken from the base of the stool where possible, these being known as 'basal cuttings'.

The preparation of the cuttings

Take the sharp blade of a knife and cut off the growth, preferably just below the surface of the soil or peat so as to include a small portion of the blanched part which, of course, always lies at the base of the growth where the sunshine cannot get at it. Be sure that the stool was watered a few hours before so that the cutting is saturated with water and the leaves are really turgid. The cutting, which should be not more than 2 inches long, should then be defoliated to about half its length and should be cut with the sharp blade just below a node.

Some gardeners allow the shoots of varieties that throw few cuttings to grow to about 5 inches in length before they cut them. They then remove the top $2\frac{1}{2}$ inches as a cutting and allow the base of the original growth left on the old stool to produce laterals at the leaf axil, and thus further cuttings are made available.

Striking the cuttings

The great thing is to try and get the cutting to root as quickly as possible, for contrary to popular belief, it is not a good thing to allow the leaves to wilt excessively. Therefore, by removing two-thirds of the leaves of the cutting, one reduces the loss of water by transpiration. The leaves should always be trimmed off close to the stem with a sharp knife. If the cuttings can be shaded after they have been dibbled into the boxes by means of being covered with a sheet of brown paper, less unnecessary transpiration takes place. Further, it undoubtedly helps to keep the atmosphere in the greenhouse or frame both close and moist. Start then with a cutting that is 'surfeited' with water and keep the leaves as turgid as possible during the time that the roots are being produced.

The compost for and insertion of cuttings

It definitely pays to use the John Innes Potting Compost No. 1 (see page 46) in the trays, boxes or pots into which the cuttings are going to be struck. It is convenient to use the standard seed tray which measures 14 in. by 8 in. by $2\frac{1}{2}$ in. deep. It is usual to put a little 'rough stuff', say peat or spent hops, in the bottom of the box to help with drainage and then to cover with the John Innes Potting Compost in such a way that it is firm, especially in the corners. Press this compost down with a wooden presser so that it is within $\frac{1}{2}$ inch of the top of the box – this allows for watering – and then give the surface a light sanding with coarse silver sand. It should be possible then to dibble in five rows of eight cuttings, making forty cuttings per box.

The cuttings must be inserted firmly so that there can be no movement at all. Use a blunt-ended dibber about $\frac{3}{8}$ inch in diameter and about 4 inches long. If the base of the dibber is about the measurement given, the top may be

Making a chrysanthemum cutting from a sturdy short-jointed shoot.

Removing a cutting from the old plant or stock. Note the right length and type of cutting to take.

thicker so as to make it easier to handle. Choose a piece of hard wood because such a dibber gets a great deal of wear. When the hole is made with the dibber, a small quantity of silver sand that was thrown purposely over the top of the box is then carried down to the base of the hole. This is important because it ensures a little extra drainage material on which the base of the cutting will rest. These small dibbled holes should be made 1 inch deep.

Firm each row of cuttings as they are put in position, and when the box is complete give a light watering through the fine rose of a can. This helps to settle them in and reduces the rate of transpiration in addition. Label the box immediately with the variety name of the plants, and it helps matters also if you put the date that the cuttings were inserted on the label at the same time.

The propagating house

As soon as all the cuttings have been placed into a box this, in its turn, should be placed on the staging or bench of a greenhouse where the bottom heat is about 48 to 50 deg. F. Many gardeners find it convenient to use sheets of corrugated iron for the staging, which should stand about 2 feet 6 inches above the normal soil level. The corrugated iron, in its turn, is covered with a 1-inch layer of thoroughly weathered coal ashes, and if the boxes are stood on this material about ¼ inch apart there is undoubtedly less watering to be done. Now comes the covering with sheets of paper, as was already mentioned on page 36, for about five days, and after this the cuttings may be sprayed over with clean water through a syringe, or better still, a Solo sprayer.

Be sure not to ventilate the house in any way during this time, and in fact, no air should be given until rooting has actually taken place. This will probably take three weeks, and with some varieties four. The air temperature of the house should be no higher than 45 deg. F., and preferably round about 42 or 43. The first real watering will not be given until the roots are starting to develop, say in three weeks' time from the day the cuttings were dibbled in. When watering is necessary, be quite liberal and make certain that the whole of the compost in the boxes is thoroughly soaked. It helps if the humidity of the house can be maintained during the striking period, and this can be done by syringing down the paths at night time, and if necessary at midday, and spraying some water over the hot-water pipes.

A few 'don'ts'

Don't attempt to accelerate the rooting by increasing the temperature.

Don't worry too much about flagging – it is surprising how plants recover.

Don't open the ventilators until all the plants have rooted.

Don't worry if the temperature rises above 45 deg. in January or February if this is caused by sunshine. It is when the temperature rises because of 'fire heat' that trouble may be expected.

The use of heated frames

Where the gardener has no greenhouse, the cuttings may be struck in heated frames, the boxes being placed on a cinder bed 2 or 3 inches deep put down especially for the purpose. The outside of the frame may be shaded by laying on a strip of hessian or by spraying the glass with 'Summer Cloud' or just a little muddy water. The lights are kept closed so as to prevent there being any extra air while the cuttings are striking. Some of the boxes around the outside of the frames, where the pipes are likely to be, may be drier than others and need a little watering in consequence.

Hormones for better rooting?

There should be no difficulty in rooting chrysanthemum cuttings, but those who for some reason or another find trouble may like to use one of the commercial 'hormone' preparations containing either alpha-naphthalene acetic acid or beta-indolylacetic acid. The plan is to dip the base of the cuttings in the solution made up in accordance with the maker's instructions, and then to dibble the cuttings in the compost in the normal way. There are powdered hormones that are sometimes used, and in that case the plan is to dip the cutting in water and then in the powder before dibbling it in. Hormones help to accelerate the development of roots and are often used by gardeners in cases where they try to propagate from the tips of young plants they have brought in, or from the tops of elongated cuttings which have been struck earlier and which they are 'stopping' for some reason or another.

Moving the struck cuttings

The moment all the cuttings in a box have rooted thoroughly the box should be removed to a cold frame where it can remain until planting out time comes, at the end of April or early in May in the South and perhaps a few weeks later in the North. This is, of course, in the case of the earlies.

With the lates the plan is to put the boxes into cold frames with full ventilation and to provide plenty of sacking or mats so as to give the necessary protection during freezing weather, especially at night time. Those who have room will prefer to keep the November- and late-flowering varieties in a cold house until the plants can be put out into the ground where they are to grow if they are later to be lifted in or in the case of the pot plants until they can be stood out on the standing ground.

Another method which is sometimes adopted, especially in the North for earlies, is to plant out the rooted cuttings, 4 inches square, into a frame which has been erected especially for the purpose and has been filled with a 2-inch depth of sterilised soil over a hard ash bottom, or better still, the John Innes Potting Compost No. 2 over ash. Excellent temporary frames can be made by using planks 4 inches by 1 inch in any lengths found convenient, and by placing three planks on top of one another at the back (sideways on) a depth of 12 inches is obtained, while if two planks are stood on one another in the same way, it gives you an 8-inch depth for the front of the frame. These planks could be kept in position with battens of wood driven into the ground on either side of them at regular intervals. Dutch lights can then be laid on top, and such a frame can be erected in a comparatively short time to accommodate as many plants as necessary.

For the first five days after the plants are set in the frames keep them closed and give no ventilation at all. If the weather proves sunny lift up the lights for a minute or so in the middle of the day and syringe the plants over. It is at the end of the week that plenty of ventilation can be given, unless it is actually freezing, and at this time a really good watering is necessary.

It is not long before such frames can be given full ventilation in the day time, and it does not take long to cover them up with hessian or old sacks at night time if the weather becomes excessively cold. This is what is called the 'hardening-off process' prior to planting out.

The early feeding

Sometimes struck cuttings are apt to starve when they have to be kept in their boxes for a long period and that is one of the advantages of planting them out in frames in the

Fig. 2. A plant freshly taken from the frame and ready to plant out. Breaks have already appeared in this vigorous young chrysanthemum with quite a large root.

John Innes Compost, because under these conditions they have sufficient food.

In the case of the young plants in the boxes, never allow them even to begin to starve, because once they get a check because of lack of plant food it takes them a very long time to recover. Fortunately, there are on the market liquid fertilisers such as 'Liquinure' which can easily be diluted according to the maker's instructions and which should be applied once or twice during the 'box-growing' period. Feed with the diluted liquid fertiliser after the boxes have been watered, and as it is necessary to give the solutionised feed over the leaves and this may damage the foliage, be prepared if necessary to syringe the leaves over with plain water afterwards. This, however, is a refinement which few gardeners can spare the time to carry out.

Special hints for small gardens

There may be some readers who are rather put off by the suggestion that dozens of boxes are needed, plus cold frames, for hardening off and so on, and I would therefore hasten to explain that in the case of the small garden it is a very simple matter to root the cuttings around the edge of a 5-inch pot. Such a pot should be well washed and dried and then should be filled with two handfuls of crocks to ensure perfect drainage. Over this should be placed a mixture consisting of 2 parts soil, 1 part coarse silver sand, and 1 part horticultural peat, this being pressed down so that it is within $\frac{1}{2}$ inch of the top of the pot; then sprinkle over the soil a handful of sharp silver sand, make holes with a dibber or a pencil 1 inch deep and 2 inches apart right round the inside rim of the pot, and put in the cuttings, firming them with two fingers.

When the cuttings have struck, they may be potted up into 3-inch pots in the John Innes P.C. No. 1 so that in the case of earlies they will be ready later to plant out in the open, or in the case of lates to be grown on in bigger pots.

Those with small gardens will find continuous cloches very useful because the chrysanthemums can be planted out under these towards the end of March with safety, and once

again it helps if the soil under the cloches can be made as
near the John Innes Potting Compost as possible. Some
have found it convenient and extremely helpful to have a
length of special electric cable in the soil below the cloches
so as to make certain that no frost damage can occur. The
amount of electricity used for this purpose is very small
indeed. Readers who have difficulty in carrying out this
simple soil-heating scheme may always write for advice to
the author.

CHAPTER VI

The Soil Mixture or Compost, and Feeding

ONE of the most worrying things when the writer was a student was the fact that when examination time came round, he might be expected to remember some twenty or thirty different soil mixtures, or composts, as they are usually called. Head gardeners in various parts of the country had their own pet composts for chrysanthemums, and the secret of these mixtures was often guarded with great jealousy. Commercial growers also went in for their own pet concoctions, and it was only when the John Innes Horticultural Institution started to carry out research into the subject, in 1934, that it became evident that composts could largely be standardised. All gardeners therefore are eternally grateful to Messrs W. J. C. Lawrence and J. Newell for their work on this subject, and those who are interested in obtaining further details should certainly consult the book *Seed and Potting Composts* written by these two experts.

Having discovered experimentally which were the best ingredients for composts, these research workers set about standardising the methods of preparing and using them, and it can be said, by and large, they contain seven ingredients: loam, sand, peat, and four fertilisers. The composts which are made to a standard formulæ undoubtedly economise in materials and labour and give the best possible results.

A good compost for chrysanthemums must hold sufficient moisture and yet be in such a condition as to allow the excess water to drain away. The structure should be crumbly so that plenty of air can get in. It must contain a balanced

Typical Cutting ready for insertion.

A well-rooted Cutting.

Plant stopped, showing first break.

*Natural first crown, showing bud ready
to be secured.*

Outdoor chrysanthemums sheltered from cold winds by hessian or hop-sacking. It is surprising how much protection is

supply of food, and sufficient for the needs of the plant at the time, and of course, in addition, it should be free from insect pests, fungi, weed seeds, and any harmful substances or organisms.

The soil, or loam as it is called, that is used should contain the right amount of clay so that when rubbed between the thumb and forefinger it is slightly greasy without being unpleasantly sticky. Do not use chalky loam, very light soil, very heavy clay, or even a silt. Go for what is called a medium loam. It is convenient to stack turf for a year or so, as then what is known as a turfy loam is produced which contains a certain amount of active humus. Test the loam with a B.D.H. Soil Indicator, and if necessary add carbonate of lime to bring the pH of the stack of soil up to 6.3. Some gardeners, when stacking the loam, put a little half-rotted straw or strawy manure between each layer in order to ensure that the biological content of the loam is right. Before using this rotted loam it must be sterilised to get rid of the pests, diseases and weed seeds (see page 49).

The peat used must be what is called horticultural peat – this is fibrous and must not be dusty. There should be a preponderance of particles $\frac{1}{8}$ inch in size. Never use a peat which contains silt and sand. The pH should be between 4 and 5 and it is useful to test it first with a B.D.H. Soil Indicator. Horticultural peat need not be sterilised.

The sand must be coarse and lime-free. It should be free of salt, organic matter, or silt. Curiously enough, few of the horticultural sands sold in this country are sufficiently coarse. The particles should grade evenly from fine up to $\frac{1}{8}$ inch in size, and a good sand would contain about 40 per cent particles of about $\frac{1}{16}$ inch.

The carbonate of lime used in the compost is really ground chalk or ground limestone, and it has been proved that this gives better results on the whole than hydrated lime. Never mix this ground chalk with any fertilisers before mixing it in with the compost.

The John Innes Base which is mixed with the John Innes Potting Compost consists of 2 parts by weight of hoof and horn, 2 parts by weight of superphosphate, and 1 part by weight of sulphate of potash – thus giving an analysis of nitrogen 5.1, soluble phosphoric acid 7.2, and potash 9.7. The nitrogen content of the hoof and horn should be 13 per cent, and it should consist of $\frac{1}{8}$-inch grist, i.e. avoid the coarse grades. The superphosphate used should contain 18 per cent phosphates, and sulphate of potash 48 per cent potash.

Formulæ

Now we come to the actual formulæ which will be used for chrysanthemums.

(*a*) The Seed Compost:

This consists of:

    2 parts by bulk loam,
    1 part by bulk horticultural peat,
    1 part by bulk coarse silver sand.

To each bushel of the above mixture add $\frac{3}{4}$ oz. of ground chalk and $1\frac{1}{2}$ oz. of superphosphate.

(*b*) The Potting Compost:

This consists of:

    7 parts by bulk loam,
    3 parts by bulk horticultural peat,
    2 parts by bulk coarse silver sand.

To each bushel of the above mixture add $\frac{1}{4}$ lb. of John Innes Base and $\frac{3}{4}$ oz. ground chalk.

NOTE: A bushel equals 2,200 cubic inches, and may be measured in a box 22 in. by 10 in. by 10 in.

A bushel of compost will fill one hundred 3-inch pots, or nine 2½-inch boxes for cuttings.

A bushel of compost is also sufficient for filling forty-five 4½-inch pots.

Mixing the compost

Sterilise the loam, sieve it through a ⅜-inch sieve and then spread it in a layer 6 inches deep. Water the horticultural peat through the fine rose of a can and spread it over the loam, and then put most of the sand on top of the peat. Mix the remainder of the sand, which must be dry, with the fertilisers and then add the ground chalk. Spread this mixture over the top of the sand. Now use a clean spade, which should preferably have been sterilised first in a 2 per cent solution of formalin, to mix the composts thoroughly. Try to keep the heap flat during the mixing so as to be able to spread the ingredients thoroughly, and then use at the end of twenty-four hours. Once the compost has been made, it must be completely used up before the end of eight weeks. After this it will be too acid.

Using the correct compost for each job

For actually striking the cuttings use the J.I. Potting Compost No. 1 plus, of course, the layer of silver sand over the top of each box.

When planting the struck cuttings into frames, into boxes, or into their first pots, use the J.I. Potting Compost No. 1 also.

When potting on from the 3-inch pots into 6-inch pots, use the J.I. Potting Compost No. 2 – that means adding two doses of the John Innes Base per bushel instead of one plus 1½ oz. ground chalk.

When potting on the plants into the final pots in which the chrysanthemums are going to flower, use the John

Innes Potting Compost No. 3 – that means adding three doses of the John Innes Base per bushel plus 2¼ oz. ground chalk.

NOTE: When the author refers to J.I.P. No. 1 in future it will mean the normal John Innes Potting Compost with one dose of John Innes Base and ground chalk. J.I.P. 2 means that there will be two doses of John Innes Base and ground chalk, J.I.P. 3 contains three doses of John Innes Base and ground chalk, and J.I.P. 4 four doses.

Mr J. B. Stevenson, the famous chrysanthemum grower, of Colham Green Nurseries, Hillingdon, uses the J.I.P. 2 for the 3-inch pots and the J.I.P. 3 for the 4½-inch pots, and J.I.P. 4 for the final 8-inch or 10-inch pots. Further, he finds it impossible to sift all the compost through a ⅜-inch sieve because of the time it takes, but remember he has to cope with some 3,000 bushels or more.

Purchasing the materials

Any gardener, be he amateur or professional, ought to be able to buy all the necessary materials for making up these John Innes Composts. There are many people, however, who do not want to go to the bother of mixing up these composts themselves, and they will find it possible to buy the John Innes Potting Compost by the bushel or the hundredweight, already made up. These composts usually arrive a little bit on the dry side so as to save weight in transport, but it does not take long to get them into the right condition by moistening them through the fine rose of a can.

Even where, on the score of expense, it is not desired to buy the whole of the compost already made up it is certainly a good plan to buy the John Innes Base already prepared, and readers who have any difficulty in obtaining the fully made-up compost or the base can always write to the author for addresses, but he would value the compliment of a stamped addressed envelope.

To sterilise some loam

Commercial growers naturally have quite big structures in which loam can be sterilised. A gardener finds it convenient to sterilise soil by the bucketful in a copper of boiling water. The loam is placed into a bucket. This is fitted with a lid, and a potato the size of an egg is buried in the centre 1 inch down. The bucket is then suspended from a bar so that the water reaches to within 1 inch of the top, and the water is boiled until the potato in the earth is thoroughly cooked.

Another method is to use a copper and pour about two gallons of water into the bottom and then to place, 2 inches above this, a perforated wooden framework which fits snugly into the sides of the copper and yet allows steam to percolate through. It is on to this framework that a perforated bucket is placed filled with the loam to be sterilised. A fire is lit below, the water boils, and the soil in the bucket then gets heated to a temperature of 210 deg. F. When it has been at this temperature for half an hour or forty minutes it should be sterilised. It is necessary in this case to use an efficient 'tested' thermometer and always to keep the lid of the copper in position to prevent the steam from escaping.

Feeding the plants

It is always extremely difficult to write about feeding any plants, and particularly so about chrysanthemums. Of course, the expert always seems to know when plants need a little extra help, and no amount of reading can take the place of practical experience. It is most important also to treat plants as individuals. Beginners can never 'see the wood for the trees'. Try, therefore, to do two things: (1) to start with the right John Innes Compost which will promote first-class root action; and (2) to give individual

D

plants extra food before they start to show starvation symptoms. The writer has great faith in what may be called homœopathic doses. It is much better to feed a little and often, than to give big doses and then forget about the plants altogether.

The old-fashioned gardener too often relied on queer concoctions which he called 'cow tea'. The idea was to use this 'tea' when it was light brown in colour as if this gave any indication at all as to its manurial content. Fortunately, today there is no need to use the old-fashioned hit-and-miss methods, for it is possible to buy liquid feeds such as Liquinure all ready made up and ready for dilution, and what is more, containing the plant foods suitable for chrysanthemum growing in the right proportions. Liquinure, it is said, is largely organic in origin, and compost-minded folk will appreciate this.

Use this liquid plant food in accordance with the directions given on the bottle, and this usually means about four tablespoonfuls per $2\frac{1}{2}$-gallon can full of water. Do not use water from tanks that are dirty and uncared for – the writer so often finds these in old greenhouses, and they are often infected with disease organisms.

For the outdoor early-flowering chrysanthemums it is convenient to use about a quarter of a gallon of the diluted Liquinure per plant once every three weeks from, say, the beginning of June until flowering time.

For the chrysanthemums that are going to be 'lifted in' to the greenhouses, feed in a similar manner, but stop feeding the moment the blooms show their colour. Two months before 'lifting in' switch over to the Liquinure containing a high percentage of potash so as to try and get the leaves nice and hard at the time the plants are carried into the greenhouse.

Pot plants

As soon as the chrysanthemums have been established about three weeks in their final pots, start to feed with diluted Liquinure, applying this every ten days. In the case of 8-inch pots it will probably be necessary to give a pint of feed on each occasion.

Automatic feeding

There are special adaptors which may be fitted to an ordinary garden hose so that exactly the right quantity of Liquinure may be sucked in as the water passes through, and thus the gardener finds it possible to feed and water at the same time and to deal with hundreds of plants in a matter of a few minutes. These automatic diluters are well worth considering by those who wish to grow chrysanthemums to perfection and who are going to feed properly and regularly.

Some people have said that a product like Liquinure is more expensive to use than a dry fertiliser, but if this were true the great advantage surely is that the feed is given with the water and so a tremendous amount of time is saved. Furthermore, it is given when it is needed and exactly in the form that the plant roots can use. Those who adopt liquid manuring invariably get better blooms.

Feeding for cuttings

It may sound most peculiar for the author to advise gardeners to feed their plants after the flowers have been cut, but it does pay, and especially so in the case of the early-flowering chrysanthemums. Here the blooms may be cut in July or August, or even early September, and the stools may not be dug up until October or early November. The danger is that the beginner leaves his plants in the border or in the cut-flower rows to get rather weedy and uncared for. After all, they have finished flowering and it appears that they are of little value.

The keen gardener, however, will take quite a different view. He knows that if he keeps the plants growing properly, they will produce him better cuttings for next year. He therefore feeds with Liquinure, after a really good hoeing and cleaning, say in September, aiming to give about a pint of diluted liquid food per plant. The result of this feeding is earlier cuttings, better cuttings, as well as more cuttings, and therefore I recommend the idea strongly.

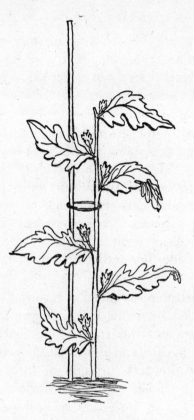

Fig. 3. Breaks growing from leaf axils in early summer, after having had the natural break bud on main stem removed.

CHAPTER VII

Stopping, Timing and Bud Securing

THERE have been far too many gardeners in the past who have tried to make a secret of this craft. The man who won innumerable prizes at the show was apt to keep his 'secrets' to himself, and thus over a period of years there has been built up what may be called 'the mystery of stopping'. There is no mystery about it at all It is just common sense, but as it is not possible to lay down hard-and-fast rules a newcomer has to learn much by experience.

The author was first made aware of the keen interest that both professional gardeners and amateurs had in stopping and timing when as a young man in 1924 he went to serve as Horticultural Adviser to the Cheshire County Council. At the Cheshire School of Agriculture, where he also taught, a number of experiments were being carried out on the early-flowering varieties. Northerners had, and still have, their own difficulties because frosts are earlier, and very often all the outside chrysanthemums are ruined by September 25th.

Now here the timing is aimed at ensuring that the plants flower earlier. The gardener need not wait for the natural break; he anticipates this by pinching out the growing point on a certain date, and as a result the particular variety concerned is in flower a fortnight or three weeks earlier than it would be if left to its own devices. May I quote here one or two dates to show what I mean.

Variety	Natural Break	Flowered	Stopped	Flowered
Almirante . . .	June 15	Sept. 30	May 20	Aug. 25
Daydream . .	June 8	Sept. 26	May 29	Sept. 3
Hurricane . . .	June 12	Sept. 27	May 31	Sept. 10
Sanctity . . .	June 15	Sept. 25	May 20	Sept. 1
September Glory .	June 15	Sept. 25	May 20	Sept. 1
September Red . .	June 10	Sept. 30	May 30	Sept. 10

It will be seen, therefore, that by stopping, or as we can say by anticipating nature's method of causing branches to develop, the gardener can ensure that his plants flower earlier. This may be very important indeed to the northerner.

Take the cut-flower grower as an example: he wants to get his blooms to market early before an outside frost has ruined them, and so if he 'times' he can get his blooms into market 'in time'.

Southern gardeners are, of course, at a great advantage because generally speaking they can get their plants out into the border earlier, and in addition because of a better climate and shorter days on the whole, the plants flower earlier. As a rule, it can be said that the very early varieties are stopped earlier than the normal earlies. Here are some more examples:

Variety	Usual Date Stopped	Average Flowering Date
Arnhem . . .	May 21	Aug. 5
Bronze McLeod .	May 19	Aug. 4
Christine Sweetheart .	May 27	Aug. 3
Edensor . . .	May 21	Aug. 9
Firedrake . . .	May 27	Aug. 5
George McLeod .	May 19	Aug. 4
Red McLeod . .	May 21	Aug. 4

Some even come into flower in July as a result of stopping, e.g.:

Variety	Usual Date Stopped	Average Flowering Date
Betty Riley. . .	May 27	July 23
Bronze Sweetheart .	May 21	July 15
Egerton Sweetheart .	May 27	July 19
Ladybower . .	May 21	July 23
Pearl Sweetheart .	May 27	July 22
Red Sweetheart . .	May 21	July 15
Sparkler . . .	May 27	July 29
Sweetheart . .	May 27	July 15

Now it does not mean to say that every variety must be stopped every year; sometimes plants will break happily on their own sufficiently early to satisfy the gardener. It is therefore the job of the grower to try to learn all he can about the varieties he is growing so that he can determine when he really must stop because the plants have not broken naturally. Another example may emphasise this point:

One year three varieties were growing side by side – Tibshelf Glory, Tibshelf Orange, and Tibshelf Shell. It seemed that they all had an equally good start – well-fed stools, early-struck cuttings and an early planting out in frames. Yet by June 2nd only Tibshelf Glory had broken naturally and so the other two were stopped. As a result, Tibshelf Shell was in flower on July 19th, Orange on the 27th, and the Glory on August 12th.*

It can truthfully be said that most normal early varieties will give a sufficient number of breaks if left to grow naturally, but there is no doubt that the lower breaks or shoots produce the longer branches, and this is quite an important factor. Generally speaking, stopping is done when the plants are out in the open ground, but northerners who plant later often have to stop in the frame.

Two stops

There are one or two exceptions to the rule, and these must be mentioned. In the first place, it is sometimes necessary to stop earlies twice. Here the idea is to try to produce dwarfer plants from the naturally taller varieties. The first stop is usually made in the frames, and as a result at planting-out time you have a sturdy chrysanthemum with three good shoots. A fortnight after planting, these shoots are stopped, and so, say, nine branches are produced which flower but seldom give as good blooms as from the one-stopping method.

This is one of the facts that is brought out so clearly in J. B. Stevenson's little book mentioned on page 10.

Tall growers

Some gardeners are impatient, and when they see a variety like Sweetheart growing taller and taller without breaking they feel they must stop. Actually, Sweetheart may grow over 1 foot high without showing any signs of breaking, and then when it does all is well. It is quite a good plan to stop such a variety after the breaks have developed. Never slaughter such a plant, i.e. cut it down hard as some have done to make it break, or you may only get two or three branches and then, to get any crop at all, you will be forced to stop again and so delay the flowering.

Stopping the second earlies

It is very difficult to know exactly what one means by a second early, but generally speaking a gardener refers to the varieties which flower in October just a little bit too late to be grown perfectly out of doors without any covering at all, a variety which it may be necessary to lift and to replant in a greenhouse where there is just a little heat to keep out frost.

We can take it, then, that in the North a frost may be expected about September 20th, and in the South about October 5th. Therefore, our second earlies must be given protection by one of the means outlined in Chapter IX. As to the stopping and, if necessary, second stopping, this depends to a certain extent on the varieties. Many of these second early kinds break naturally. They have a little longer period in which to grow in, and if they are allowed to grow normally without being stopped at all they do quite well. In the chart below will be found a number of varieties which the author usually finds quite unnecessary to 'time' at all.

Variety	Natural Break or Stop	Second Stopping	Average Flowering Date
Balcombe Flame . .	Nat. break	None	Oct. 19
Blanche du Poitou . .	May 15	None	Oct. 10
Celebrity . . .	Nat. break	None	Oct. 14
Constance Baker . .	Nat. break	None	Oct. 28
Dora Ramsey . . .	Nat. break	None	Oct. 26
Edith Alston . . .	Nat. break	None	Oct. 6
Elegance . . .	May 12	None	Oct. 8
Enid Goffe . . .	Nat. break	None	Oct. 24
Golden Mary Elizabeth .	April 20	None	Oct. 2
Jean Pattison . . .	May 10	None	Oct. 20
Market Gold . . .	Nat. break	None	Oct. 15
Mary Elizabeth . .	April 21	None	Oct. 2
Pearl Loveliness . .	Nat. break	None	Oct. 19
Ryecroft White . .	Nat. break	None	Oct. 15
Snowdon . . .	May 6	None	Oct. 19
Yellow Wallace . .	Nat. break	None	Oct. 13

Stopping the lates

I suppose that the outstanding feature in connection with the earlies is the fact that they almost all of them give their best blooms when these are allowed to appear on the first buds. Therefore, you either grow them with one stopping or allow them to break naturally. In the case of the second earlies the main feature seems to be that most varieties do well when allowed to break naturally. With the pot varieties or the lates, as they are so often called, there is a great deal of second stopping done, and the list which appears later, on page 63, demonstrates what I mean.

With all kinds and types of chrysanthemums it is extremely important to grow good plants, and with the lates it is equally important to ensure that the cuttings are struck early. In fact, most gardeners see that the cuttings of the lates are struck long before the earlies – contrary to popular belief. It will be seen in Chapter X that the pot variety or

late spends the majority of its life, as its classification suggests, 'in a pot', therefore the first stopping is done as a rule
when the plants are in their $4\frac{1}{2}$- or 5-inch pots, and in fact
it is convenient and advisable to do the pinching out of the
growing points as soon as the chrysanthemum plant is
really happy and established in this size pot. Do not do the
first stopping, whatever you do, while the plants are still
growing in their 60's, i.e. the 3-inch pots, the idea being
that the stopping must be done when the plants are growing
happily and freely.

The next important point is that stopping is not done
until the plants are starting to produce their side growths
naturally. If the gardener cuts off the growing tip of a late
with the idea of forcing the side branches to develop, then
what usually happens is that one or two strong laterals
develop towards the top of the stem and then a number of
weaker ones lower down the stem. A good grower wants
all the breaks to be equally strong, he dislikes one-sided
plants with some branches early and others later, some
stronger and others weaker.

Pinch out, then, the growing point of the plants the
moment the side growths are seen to be developing in the
axils of the leaves, and this should be, if you time the
potting on carefully, as I have said above, when the plants
are in their $4\frac{1}{2}$- or 5-inch pots. When the laterals are clearly
developing the gardener must make up his mind as to how
many of these he will retain. Generally speaking, it will be
the four strongest, which are evenly spaced around the
stem.

Second stopping

In time these side growths will develop and will themselves start to throw out what may be called sub-laterals,
and when this happens the second stopping can safely take

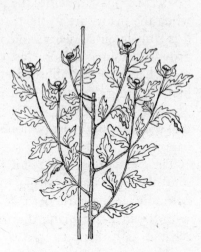

Fig. 4. *Six breaks ready for dis-budding. Buds should be rubbed out as indicated, leaving a single bud on each break to develop, thereby form-ing the first crown buds.*

Fig. 5. *Six breaks with first crown buds fully secured and developing.*

place. Here it is important only to pinch out a very small piece at the very tip of the growth. Do not use a knife. Do not cut away any fully expanded leaf. Use a nice sharp thumb nail and just nip out the actual growing point. Probably this second stopping will take place five or six weeks after the first one, and in very rare cases in exactly a month.

The second stopping or timing will, of course, be when the plants are in their flowering pots, normally 8-inch or even 10-inch. There are occasions when one has to adopt unusual methods. Take, for example, the plant which has been allowed to break naturally or which has been stopped and then produces, say, three good strong leading shoots and some weaker laterals lower down. The grower may want to get his eight flowers or so, and thus he stops the top three laterals, and as a result two blooms will be produced per side branch. He can thus cause a shy cropper to produce more blooms.

It never pays to try to make things difficult. If a plant will grow naturally without any stopping at all, let it do so and be thankful. If a plant crops at the wrong time of the year and it suits your purpose to stop it and make it flower earlier or later as the case may be, by all means stop it. The great thing is to experiment when one becomes a chrysanthemum enthusiast, and to grow three plants of a variety side by side. Let one grow naturally, stop the next plant once, stop the next plant twice, and by the end of the season you will know far more about that variety for your own particular conditions than anyone else. Some varieties like

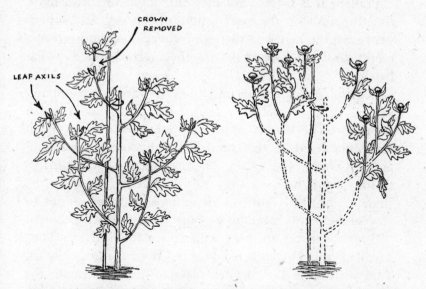

Fig. 6. First crown buds removed, enabling second crown buds to appear in leaf axils. The second break can be regulated by removing some of these axils.

Fig. 7. Eight buds have been allowed to develop on six second crown breaks. Four of the second breaks have (see Fig. 6) not been allowed to grow.

Crensa always seem to have weak-necked first crowns but nice strong necks on the second crowns.

The disadvantage of a second stopping is that the plants may flower too late. Take the variety Friendly Rival as an example. We always grow it on its first crowns, but when we tried stopping it a second time it missed the Christmas market altogether and was in flower in February. On the other hand, that lovely white variety Favourite, which we grow so much, always comes too early if we only stop it once, and when we take it on its second crown bud we get the flowers in for the Christmas market when the prices are high. As a matter of fact, this is one of the varieties which will break naturally twice and so has to have very little special treatment.

Perhaps it is true to say that one ought to spend more time on studying the exact timing of the second stopping than even the first, and therefore, chrysanthemum growers ought to keep a diary where they record exactly what happens in each case. The keen expert is the one who anticipates the natural second break and does the stopping, say, a week or ten days before the plant would break naturally. The danger of not stopping soon enough, on the other hand, is that the plant will not produce long enough stems, and so the gardener keeps an eye on this factor, and if he finds that from his second stopping the branches are too short, he determines in future either to stop earlier or to make his blooms on first crowns.

Some lecturers are very arbitrary in their advice. They say, for the November flowerers stop the majority of varieties during the first few days of June, and with the December kinds do the stopping first of all in mid-April and then in mid-June. A few varieties will be found in the list below which will give a fair picture as to the normal possibilities with pot plants as a whole.

Variety	Natural Break or Stop	Second Stopping	Average Flowering Date
American Beauty . .	April 17	June 14	Dec. 12
Agnes Ford . . .	April 19	June 18	Dec. 20
Baldock's Crimson . .	April 21	June 18	Dec. 22
Bronze Rose . . .	April 18	June 15	Dec. 13
Cream Monument . .	April 20	June 20	Dec. 15
Fernleigh Beauty . .	April 16	June 13	Dec. 9
Friendly Rival . .	June 7	None	Dec. 4
Imperial Pink . . .	April 18	June 11	Dec. 17
Jane Ingamells . .	April 19	June 12	Dec. 15
Monument . . .	April 20	June 20	Dec. 15
Rose Harrison. . .	April 18	June 14	Dec. 14
Sussex Bronze . .	April 17	June 16	Dec. 18
White Rose . . .	April 17	June 14	Dec. 16
Yellow American Beauty .	April 21	June 16	Dec. 11

Bud securing

It used to be the custom to refer to 'taking the bud', but gradually this term was confused with stopping, and so experts started to apply the words 'securing the bud' to the particular operation concerned. This securing of the bud is merely a question of disbudding or dis-shooting. One disbuds a rose by removing the little side-flowering buds near the apex of the shoot, thus leaving the terminal bud to bloom alone, and you get one good rose per stem in consequence instead of a cluster of smaller blooms. In the case of the chrysanthemum the grower looks for the 'terminal bud' very carefully, and the moment it appears he is anxious to give it every chance to develop properly, and so any lateral growths that develop just below this bud are removed as well as any other little flower buds that are seen. It is this operation of clearing out of the way any growths that may compete with the end flower bud which is called 'securing the bud'.

The bud may be very small and it will not be long before

it draws away from the crown of leaves which surround it, and when this happens, any competing growths or flower buds must be carefully pinched off. It is surprising how little laterals or tiny buds will rob the end or 'terminal' flower bud, and therefore at the right period of the year growers must be constantly on the look-out so that the buds are 'secured' early enough. If a bud is secured too late, it may produce a bloom with a daisy eye, it may develop a flower of poor colour and shape, and in fact all kinds of things may happen when the securing is not done early enough. Those who grow for the big November shows say that buds must be secured round about August 15th. They start, therefore, to watch their plants carefully from August 10th.

Mr Keith Luxford's 'timing' suggestions

Fortunately, the Horticultural Training Centre at Thaxted is very close to Mr Keith Luxford's famous nursery at Sawbridgeworth. Mr Luxford is the well-known chrysanthemum expert, and the author was indeed fortunate in getting him to write these special notes on timing for the benefit of exhibitors.

As has already been said in the earlier parts of this book, the actual date of flowering of chrysanthemums undoubtedly can be influenced by the time that the cuttings are rooted and the date on which the plants are stopped. Other influences include the climate of the district where the plants are growing, and the actual weather of that particular season. It is as well, however, to have some tables of guidance, and Mr Luxford has kindly provided these, which may be taken as representative for gardeners who are growing chrysanthemums in the southern half of Great Britain. Northern growers may have to stop fourteen days earlier to get similar results.

SHIRLEY BRILLIANT

Decoratives

The reflexed and incurving varieties should be stopped twice, the first time during April, and the second time about the third week of June, for November flowering. These varieties are best rooted in early February. For exhibition grow about six blooms per plant. Take up three strong shoots from the first stop, and two on each of these from the second stop.

Decoratives for Christmas flowering are treated in the same way as November flowering, except that the second stop takes place at about July 10th to 15th, and the next bud secured; this should form about the end of October or early November.

Singles, anemones and pompons

These require to be rooted about mid-February to early March and given cold treatment throughout. Just enough heat to keep away frost is all that is necessary. Plant out towards the end of April in the South. Stop once only for exhibition in the first week of June.

Take up four to six shoots to the next bud and secure. This should form about the third week of July.

If for cutting purposes, two stops should be made, the first about the end of May, and the second mid- to end of June, according to the strength of the plants.

Medium exhibition varieties (those which flower in November)

These varieties are not large enough to be shown in Section I, but may be shown in Section IV. They require stopping about April 14th. Take up three shoots to the next bud. Buds should form about the end of August. This applies to the following varieties:

E

Bronze Mona Davis	Crimson Mona Davis
Edward Page	Elegance
Golden Mary Elizabeth	Mary Elizabeth
Mona Davis	Red Mona Davis
Rose Mona Davis	Salmon Strauss
White Elegance	White Mona Davis
Yellow Edward Page	Yellow Mona Davis

Large exhibition varieties

These should be rooted during the first half of January. Secure natural first crown buds. Rub out the first bud that appears, which is the break bud. Take up two strong shoots to the next bud and secure. If this bud should form before or about the end of July rub out and run on to the next, this being second crowns. Most varieties only make a short break from the first crown to the second. This bud should be in plenty of time for November shows. It is very seldom necessary to run on to second crowns, but early first crown buds are very difficult to open. First crown buds should form about August 10th to 20th. Some of the most popular varieties are:

Archie Woolman	Birmingham
Candeur	Dida Bryant
Geoffrey Philippe	F. E. Luxford
H. E. Trueman	Golden Trueman
Mrs R. C. Pulling	Mary Cameron
Pockett's Maroon	Primrose Candeur
Shirley Amber	Shirley Masterpiece
Shirley Triumph	Sybil Molyneaux

Large exhibition varieties (November show) (that require stopping for first crowns, in order to get them in time for November shows)

After stopping take up two shoots to the next bud and secure. These varieties require to be rooted in the first half of December. Varieties requiring this treatment are:

Variety				Stopping time
Alfred Simpson .	.	.	.	mid-April
Comrade .	.	.	.	early May
Flo Reed .	.	.	.	early May
Gordon Habgood	.	.	.	mid-March
Hugh Mitchell .	.	.	.	end February
Jas. Bryant.	.	.	.	end February
Joyce Richards .	.	.	.	early May
Linella .	.	.	.	early May
Majestic .	.	.	.	early May
Mrs H. Habgood	.	.	.	mid-March
Purple Prince .	.	.	.	mid-April
Red Majestic	.	.	.	early May
Rise of Day .	.	.	.	mid-April
R. Richardson .	.	.	.	mid-April
Yellow Majestic .	.	.	.	early May

Large exhibition incurving

This section is becoming very popular owing to the form and keeping qualities. Most varieties require to be grown on natural first crowns. If any of the varieties have not shown the break bud by the end of May, pinch out small point of the plant to enable it to break to be in time for securing the buds by August 1st.

Exhibition incurved

Cuttings are best rooted towards the end of December, and in quite a number of varieties are best grown on second crowns. Secure buds first week in September or thereabouts, and they should be ready for early to mid-November shows. Grow three blooms per plant. Varieties which can be grown on first crowns are:

Buttercup	Coronation Gold
Godfrey's Eclipse	Ondine
Romance	Shirley Buff
Wolverine	Yellow Ondine

Varieties which require stopping mid-May and secure first crown buds are:

Advancement	Bronze Progress
Chas. Hopkinson	Lord Somers
Mrs K. L. Southam	Progress
White Progress	Yellow Progress

Varieties which can be grown on second crown buds are:

Captain Kettle	Charles Curtis
Edith Laundy	Mrs S. Dove
Red Harrison	

NOTE: In all cases stopping means pinching out the smallest point of the main stem to enable the plant to break into growth before the break bud is allowed to form.

CHAPTER VIII

Earlies Out of Doors

THERE is definitely a far greater interest displayed throughout the country in early varieties than in lates. Any one with a garden can grow 'earlies', but it needs a heated greenhouse and lots of pots to grow Christmas-flowering kinds. Here we have a plant that is grown successfully all over England; in fact, it is probably true to say that there are many more enthusiastic growers in the North than in the South.

Soil

A good chrysanthemum soil would seem to be one of friable medium loam, say at least 15 inches deep. It should be prepared in the late autumn by thorough digging in order to bury the manure or compost to be added. Most gardeners bastard trench, but there are some experts, especially those on heavy soil, who claim that single-digging is quite adequate.

It seems that chrysanthemums do best on soil with a pH of 6.5, i.e. a soil which is slightly acid. Therefore always test the soil, after digging it over, with a B.D.H. Soil Indicator.

Manuring

It is surprising what heavy dressings of dung or well-rotted compost chrysanthemums need. The best flowers the author ever grew were on land manured with well-rotted dung at 75 tons to the acre, and there are commercial growers who attempt to use 80 tons per acre, and this works out at about 36 lb. per square yard. So be generous with the bulky organic manure used.

In addition, use an organic fertiliser such as hoof and horn, or fish, to which has been added potash so as to produce a formula as advised on page 46.

Liming

Only give lime if necessary and in accordance with the reaction shown by the B.D.H. Indicator. Carbonate of lime is usually applied as a top dressing as the surface is raked level. Many gardeners use $\frac{1}{2}$ lb. per square yard as a routine dressing.

Planting

The carefully raised plant which is now growing well in its frame (see page 39) and is fully hardened off is now ready for planting. In order to give it a perfect start a good watering and feed with Liquinure may be given the day before. As a result, when the plant is got out of the soil with a trowel (so as to ensure a good ball of soil to the roots) it will be in fine fettle and should not droop or look back after planting.

In the mixed flower border the plants may go in in drifts or groups of eight to twelve plants, or even four or five plants in the case of small gardens.

For cut-flower purposes it is convenient to plant them in straight rows as this makes for ease of cultivation, especially for those who use some type of mechanical cultivator. With good soil it is as well to have the rows 15 inches apart, and then, after four rows, to allow a 2-foot wide path. You can then easily pick all the blooms in the cut-flower bed from the path – without having to tread on it at all.

Another method I have adopted with success in the North is to have the rows 1 foot apart and arrange five rows to the 4-foot bed, the two outside rows being right on the edge of the bed in consequence. In the North the plan, very often, is to cover these beds with glass lights 5 feet by 4 feet when it comes to, say, September 20th. Then with the lights over the bed held in place by temporary 'scaffolding' and hessian hung all around the bed, it is possible to keep the plants cropping longer. I have even used a few lighted candles down the paths at night time, and it is surprising how many degrees of frost candles will keep out (see page 81).

Yet a third method is to have the rows 18 inches apart, and then four rows will fit into the 5-foot bed – in this case the plants in the rows are 1 foot apart. The temporary paths can always be wider if necessary. I have had them 2 feet 8 inches wide. This does make it easier to carry out all the disbudding necessary in the rows as well as the picking and carrying away the blooms you have cut. Remember, this bed may be anything from 10 feet to 100 feet long, and you may arrange to have four different varieties to a bed, one row of each; or, on a larger scale, the one variety only; or even, in a very small garden, twenty or thirty varieties and only three or four plants of each, but all planted in the serried lines. Have the rows north and south if you can.

When to plant

Plant when the soil is right, i.e. not too sticky and wet, and then you will be able to plant firmly, and this is so important. It is impossible to firm 'squishy' muddy land.

Plant, too, as soon as you can after the third week of April in the South and about the end of the second week of May in the Midlands. Northerners often have to wait until the third or fourth week of May. Planting times may differ from East to West just as much as from North to

South. I know of some very warm spots on the west coast of Scotland and some very cold areas on the east coast of England! So plant in accordance with the general scheme, modifying it to your own conditions.

If you plant too early there is always a danger that the plants may be cut down by the frost. Some keen growers therefore keep a batch of continuous cloches 'up their sleeves' and use them for chrysanthemums. They can then plant in April with safety and pop the cloches over, and then when all fear of frost is past, say at the end of May, the cloches can be removed. It is an expensive way of using cloches, however, unless you can fit this idea into a 'strip scheme' (see *ABC of Cloches*, by the same author). Many chrysanthemum experts say that it is worth it in order to be certain.

How to plant

It pays to plant with a rather flattened trowel and to make a good hole to receive the ball of soil and the roots (see page 70). An air pocket must never be permitted under the roots, and that so often happens when dibber-planting is done.

It is quite a good plan in the Eastern counties, and wherever the weather is really dry, to draw out drills as for sowing beetroot and to plant the young chrysanthemums in these. The young plants then get some shelter from the wind, and in addition, if any rain does fall, it reaches the roots quickly. Again, watering is easier to carry out when there are little furrows than when the planting is done on the flat.

It is said that a good watering at planting time helps the plants to withstand the frost, but the author has no experimental evidence to prove this. Hoe the ground over lightly two or three days after planting if the weather is dry.

Staking

Each chrysanthemum will be given a stake or bamboo sufficiently long so that the whole of the plant (i.e. within 6 inches of the blooms) may be supported if necessary. There must be 2 feet 6 inches length out of the ground in the case of some varieties and 3 feet 6 inches with others. At least 1 foot of the bamboo must be pushed into the ground to ensure good purchase. Do not have too long stakes or the flowers themselves, when they appear, may beat against them in the wind and so be spoiled.

Be sure to tie the plants loosely to the bamboos or stakes – you must leave room for the stem of the plant to swell. Most growers use raffia for this purpose, but three-ply fillis is quite suitable. I hope ere long it will be possible to use Laxtex again, which I have tried out with great success at the Horticultural Training Centre, because this gives as the stems swell.

Do not, when tying, ever crush all the flowering stems together, as otherwise the leaves will not get a chance of breathing properly, and further you will find the inside leaves turning yellow. Some, for this reason, take the trouble to use four bamboos to a plant, inserting them so that they bend outward somewhat, say at an angle of 75 degrees.

When, however, growing on the cut-flower bed principle as set out on page 71, it is an easy matter to drive into the ground, 1 foot deep, posts 4 feet 6 inches long and, say, 2 inches square, at each end of the bed. Then on to the top of these posts nail a cross-bar and run wires from one bar to the other cross-bar at the opposite end of the bed. If there are four rows, then five wires will be needed, one on either side of the bed and one in between each of the rows. It is then possible to tie three-ply fillis in between the wires so that this runs at right angles to them, and then squares are produced in between which a plant can grow perfectly.

Some gardeners have developed an even more elaborate system. They have the permanent posts at the corners of the bed, and then if this bed is no longer than, say, 50 feet, they have the wires fixed to the cross-bars at either end and the cross-bars are movable so that they can raise or lower the wires at will. They start with the cross-bars at, say, 1 foot and then as the plants grow they raise them to 2 feet, then to 3 feet, and so on. It is a simple matter to lash the cross-members to the uprights if necessary at the appropriate heights.

NOTE: The later all this staking and supporting is done the easier it is to keep the beds hoed and clean.

Stopping

The plants may have been stopped before planting out, but as a general rule this will take place after the chrysanthemums have been out a few weeks in the border. For further details see Chapter VII. It is just a question of pinching out the growing point at the right time, if it is necessary.

It is always claimed that it takes seven weeks from stopping for the flower bud to appear at the tip of the branches or breaks that develop as a result, and a further seven weeks for that bud to blossom out into a perfect flower. The time factor varies with the variety, and the keen grower treats his plants like children – each one is an individual.

There is one factor which must be borne in mind when thinking of stopping and that is that feeding does play some part in hastening or delaying the development of the flowers. Starve, and a plant will flower earlier to reproduce its own species – feed well, and you will tend to delay the production of bloom, especially if you give too much nitrogen. Phosphates help to ensure earlier flowering, and for this reason commercial chrysanthemum growers, are as a rule, liberal with bone meal.

After stopping, do make up your mind how many branches you are going to allow to develop. Some varieties will produce twelve breaks quite easily, others only five or six. Those who want exhibition blooms will only retain four breaks, and any others that arise will be cut out carefully when small. For normal work, however, aim for eight or nine good blooms and you will be very satisfied.

General cultivation

Keep down the weeds by regular hoeing along the rows and in between them, or in the border just among the plants. It is not necessary or advisable to hoe deeply; just move the top half-inch or so with a sharp Dutch hoe blade.

Watch out all the time for pests such as aphides and capsid bugs, and spray, if necessary, with nicotine (see page 169), or even H.E.T.P.

It may be necessary in the lighter soils to apply a top dressing or mulch of horticultural peat or fine well-rotted compost. Either of these is safer to use than lawn mowings, which are apt to heat up if put on too deeply and which are, of course, full of 'weed' seeds – even if only of annual meadow grass.

Top dressings

From June 1st and onwards the feeding usually commences as outlined in Chapter VI, page 49. Some prefer to use a dry feed like a balanced fish manure once a fortnight at 1 ounce or so to the square yard, while others are very pleased with the regular liquid feeds. The former have to be watered in if the weather proves droughty. It is undoubtedly at this stage that the little-and-often idea pays handsomely.

Disbudding

Those who have no desire to produce nice large specimen blooms will allow the plants to grow naturally, and then what are called 'spray' chrysanthemums are grown. Most, however, prefer the bigger flowers, and so they set about to 'secure the bud' as it is called. This means that after the first six- or seven-week period – or in the case of some varieties like McLeod after five to six weeks – the gardener concentrates on the end flower head of each branch and removes all the side buds or shoots he finds growing in the axils of the leaves.

The sooner this dis-shooting or disbudding is done, the better. Some use a sharp penknife and others just the thumb-nail. If there should be a cluster of buds at the terminal end of the branch, and there sometimes is, then retain the centre one and remove the surrounding buds. It is a curious thing, but true, that if the side buds are left too long then the main flower will tend to be flatter in shape than it should be.

All this work will be done in normal years by the end of July or before, though in late years and with varieties that tend to flower towards the end of September the work might be only completed by the end of the first week of August.

Watering

Watering is usually necessary after the end of June. It depends on the year, of course, and to a certain extent on how complete the mulching has been. Overhead irrigation is ideal, and most gardeners, if they will, can use some simple apparatus to this end, either the whirling type or the straight backwards and forwards apparatus like the Brosson, which we use at the Horticultural Training Centre with such success. Such watering has to be done as the plants seem to require it, i.e. before the leaves start to droop at all.

Pest and disease control

Watch the plants carefully, and if any trouble is seen compare the symptoms with those described in Chapter XVI and supply the remedy immediately. It is so important to be observant and thus to note any troubles in their very early stages.

Protection against frost

Even earlies are sometimes damaged by frost, especially in the North, and so various schemes may be adopted to protect the plants in late September. Such methods are described in fair detail in Chapter IX.

CHAPTER IX

Covering up or Lifting in

IT has already been suggested in Chapters VII and VIII that it is possible to grow chrysanthemums out of doors and then to cover them up where they are growing about the end of September and so give them the necessary protection, which will enable them to flower satisfactorily during the month of October or even early November. This 'covering up', as it is called, can be done by means of dutch lights, and at the Horticultural Training Centre we often move a whole 'dedutchable' house from the tomatoes, which by then have nearly finished, in order to cover the chrysanthemums and give them the necessary protection. This is a question of the mountain going to Mahomet.

Most people, however, find it more convenient to take Mahomet to the mountain, and in that case they grow the chrysanthemum plants out of doors and then, towards the end of September, they dig the plants up with a fair amount of soil to their roots and plant them in the greenhouse where they are to flower. There are, naturally, varieties which lift better than others. After all, lifting is quite a disturbing operation, and it is only to be expected that certain varieties will put up with the unusual check to the roots more than others.

It will be as well now to discuss the two methods in detail.

Covering in situ

One of the easiest methods of covering the plants is by the use of canvas, or tiffany. Posts, each 2 inches by 2 inches, are driven into the ground at intervals of, say, 10 feet right the way round the bed or beds concerned. These posts should be at least 6 feet high, so this means that they should be about 7 feet 6 inches long in the first place so as to allow about an 18-inch length in the ground. At the corners it is usual to knock in strainers, either like the stout tent pegs used for marquees which are driven in at an angle of 45 degrees 3 or 4 feet away and from which a rope or a wire is stretched to the top of the post, or instead, the straining post may be at an angle of 45 degrees, as it were, inside the bed, and is nailed to the main post at the top.

From the top of the post a galvanised wire is stretched tightly, and it is from this wire that the hessian or tiffany is hung. The screen, of course, gives protection from cold winds and from frosts. It is necessary to have a roof over which will let in the maximum amount of light. Some growers just use a butter muslin roof, others prefer to lay over the top dutch lights, or ordinary lights from a frame, to give the effect of a temporary greenhouse roof. When lights are used it is necessary to have cross-beams running from the posts instead of wires. These may be just strips of wood about 2 in. by 2 in. and the lights are prevented from sliding off either by tying the 'horns' to the cross-members or by wiring the cross-members down to the stops as in the case of dutch lights.

It is convenient sometimes to have what may be called a 'double span', that is to say, to have two beds running side by side, each one containing, say, four rows of chrysanthemums at 12 inches apart. The centre pathway between the two beds is purposely planned to be only 18 inches wide, and then the posts used for this centre pathway are driven in in such a manner that they are 6 to 8 inches higher than the posts which run on the outside of the bed. The result is that the lights can be laid in position so that they slope slightly outwards and downwards rather like the roof of an ordinary greenhouse, only far less steeply. In order to accommodate the two dutch lights which will meet at the apex, it is necessary sometimes to have a double strip of boarding nailed on either side of the central posts so that the top of each light, which will lie in juxtaposition to the next, may be attached to its own rail and so not slide off.

All this sounds very complicated in a book, but it is much easier to work out in practice and carry out on the site, especially if flat-headed fairly short nails are used, plus washers, so that the minimum of damage to the timber is done. All timber used should be treated with Cuprinol to prevent it rotting away, and it helps tremendously if the hand machine known as the Drivall is used for knocking in the posts. This Drivall ensures the minimum of damage to the top of the posts and makes it possible to drive them in without having to point them first, as well as making it unnecessary to dig holes.

Commercial growers often put up a framework which is used year after year. This may be of wood or iron. Some have rails running along the sides of the beds to which the hessian curtain is fixed. The disadvantage of this method, of course, is that the chrysanthemums have got to be grown in the same strip of land year after year and the correct rotations cannot be carried out.

It is hoped that by now the reader will have understood the principle, and that is to erect some kind of cheap structure which will allow cheap curtaining to be put right round the bed or beds and to have a temporary roof of dutch lights or butter muslin. In the case of the butter muslin, this will be unrolled during fine dry weather and can be put back at night time if the conditions seem to infer that it is going to be frosty. As to the keeping out of frost, this can be done with cheap paraffin lamps like the Zamba which are stood down the pathways every 10 feet or so. Hurricane lamps can be used, and as I said in an earlier chapter I have often kept out a number of degrees of frost by simply burning candles stuck into bottles every 6 feet or so down the pathway.

If I have given the impression that the roof needs to be very high, I must make it clear that it need only be 6 inches above the tops of the plants. The alternative to using the hessian and tiffany is to use dutch lights throughout, and in this case the plan for the normal dedutchable would be to have two beds 5 feet 6 inches wide with a path 30 inches wide down the middle. This would accommodate ten rows of chrysanthemums. These rows would be five each side of the centre path, and we plant them 13 inches apart each way in 'blocks' of twenty, leaving an 18-inch space between the blocks to facilitate disbudding, cutting, etc. These distances may seem to some to be rather a close plant, and for those who like a wider spacing, only four rows should be planted each side of the centre path at 15 inches apart, leaving 18 inches between plants in the rows and 2 feet between the blocks. The closer plant enables us to house six hundred plants in a 72-feet dedutchable. The dedutchable is normally 13 feet 6 inches wide at the base, slopes up to 10 feet wide at the top and then the two dutch lights slope upwards to form the roof, the apex of which is 7 feet above soil level. We have found at the Horticultural Training Centre that it is possible to move a 72-feet dedutchable from covering tomatoes at the end of September over the chrysanthemums some 100 yards away in eight hours, using four men.

Lifting in

The varieties that are going to be lifted into the green-

F

house are often planted in threes in a triangle, each plant being a foot away from the next, and the grower then allows 18 inches from triangle to triangle. The idea is that the grower can cut round the outsides of the triangle with a spade a fortnight or so before the actual date of lifting, with the result that the three plants come up with a really good ball of soil, and having been placed in a wheelbarrow or on to a hand truck can be taken into the greenhouse.

Other gardeners claim that this triangle method of planting is of little value because the big ball of soil which has to be lifted is far too heavy for ease of management. They claim, on the other hand, that the plants need a little more room than ordinary outdoor varieties so that they will grow hard and short-jointed. They argue that by planting closer, the chrysanthemum stems get drawn and soft. There is a lot to be said for this, and the author can therefore well recommend planting on the 20-inch square principle. It pays with varieties to be lifted to give them a single bamboo each. In rather exposed situations it is useful to drive a 6-feet 2 in. by 2 in. post into the ground about 18 inches at the end of each row and to stretch a strong wire the whole length in between. The tops of the bamboos can then be tied to this wire, and this gives extra support.

Treat the plants in a similar manner as advised for the November varieties. Give artificial rain in the summer, if it proves dry, by the use of an overhead sprinkler, and feed the plants as advised on page 50. The great thing is to see that there is plenty of potash so that the leaves are really firm. Excess of nitrogen naturally causes trouble at lifting in and afterwards.

Be most careful to control all pests and diseases, and it pays just before lifting in to spray all the plants thoroughly with a colloidal-copper wash such as Bouisol, using a good white-oil emulsion spreader in addition.

The actual lifting in is usually done early in October in the South and about September 20th in the North. Be sure to cut round the plants with a spade plunged in the full length of the blade about 6 inches away from the main stem. If this work is done fourteen days beforehand, then the roots tend to collect in the square thus prepared and the ball of soil lifts more easily. Two days before lifting give the whole area a thorough soaking with water by means of the overhead sprinkler. The balls of soil may then be planted in trenches prepared in the houses, and it is usual to start by inserting the plants in the first trench and then digging over, thus forming the second trench where another batch of plants may be put in. In the house it is usual to plant about a foot apart and every 4 feet to leave a 1-foot path so as to allow for ease of picking.

After all the plants are in give them a thorough watering, and remembering that they have been growing outside in plenty of air, see that there is plenty of ventilation night and day for the first fortnight or so at least. But for two days you can keep the house closed to check transpiration until they get over the move. There should be some pipe heat so as to keep the temperature at about 50 degrees. Beginners often think it extraordinary that the ventilators should be opened wide when the heat is on. This, of course, is the ideal method of ensuring good plants free from mildew, and good flowers which do not damp off in the centre. As the nights get colder the ventilators will be closed in the late afternoon, but a certain amount of ventilation should be given during the day unless the weather is outstandingly frosty.

Water the plants as necessary, and this will undoubtedly be so with the heat on, and feed with Liquinure once a week until the flowers start to show their colour.

In the house, with the plants growing so close together,

it is almost impossible to do any spraying or dusting to
control disease, and so it is necessary to control mildew
with one of the sulphurisers; aphides by burning the special
tobacco shreds or by the use of a nicotine vapouriser; and
capsids, caterpillars and thrips by the use of a D.D.T.
smoke 'bomb'. Any good horticultural sundriesman or
chemist should be able to supply these.

Varieties

There are a number of varieties which are particularly
suitable for lifting in, and these are listed below:

Variety	Description	Flowering Month
Avondale Beauty	A heavy cropper	Oct./Nov.
Balcombe Bronze	Has gold tipped petals	Nov./Dec.
Blanche du Poitou	Dwarf, large white flowers	Oct.
Crensa	Cerise, tipped buff	
Dorothy Wilson	Dwarf, with medium yellow flowers	Nov.
Enton Beauty	Crimson with gold reverse	Oct./Nov.
Exmouth Pink	A glorious pink	
Favourite Supreme	Bronze with pink suffusion	Dec.
Golden Seal	A lovely golden yellow	
Imperial Pink	Large reflexed blooms, brilliant rose pink shade	Dec.
Lilac Monument	Excellent form, unusual colour	Nov.
May Wallace and Apricot Wallace	Attractive pink and apricot shades, lasts well	Dec.
Mrs R. A. Roots	Excellent favourite white	Oct./Nov.
Rose Chochod	Incurved variety, deep mauvy-rose	Nov.
Shirley Late Red	Brilliant colour with semi-quilled petals	Dec.
Snowdon	Dwarf white	Oct.
Thanksgiving Pink	Fine deep colour	Dec./Jan.
Yellow Orb	Incurved variety, small leaves, thick stems	Nov.

CHAPTER X

Pot Growing in the Greenhouse

THOUGH much can be done with lifting plants out of the soil in the open ground and bringing them into the greenhouse for planting there, no one could suggest that this is by any means as satisfactory as growing the plants in pots. Furthermore, though as a general rule for the sake of economy, some varieties are lifted in in this way, most gardeners agree that the lifting-in method is far more suitable for the October and early November varieties, and is not really worth while for the late flowering kinds. The great advantage of growing chrysanthemums in pots is that it ensures, or should ensure, the regular steady growth which makes for the best type of bloom.

There are three kinds of pots usually bought by gardeners: (1) the normal clay pots; (2) a new type of plastic pot, which is a little dearer but has the advantage of being almost unbreakable; and (3) the concrete pot, which I used with great success in the North and which I am told is much liked in the Channel Islands. Some gardeners have been able to buy 'throw-out' square biscuit tins and there has been no difficulty in knocking a small hole or two in the bottom of these to ensure good drainage. After all, the whole thing is that the plant should be able to grow in a container which is large enough to ensure perfect growth, light enough so that it can easily be lifted into the greenhouse, and sturdy enough so that it does not fall to pieces.

In Chapter V we dealt with the raising of the plants, and in the case of the semi-late and late-flowering varieties the idea is to get the well-struck cuttings into their 3-inch pots during the third and fourth week of February. Gardeners who do this can make sure that the young plants are not too elongated and leggy. The J.I.P. Compost No. 2 should be used, and this should be filled into the pots around the roots of the plants fairly loosely. There should only be one concave crock at the bottom of the pot, for with loose potting one never needs excessive drainage. It pays to ensure that the pots are quite clean, and many gardeners take the precaution of soaking them in boiling water before use, that is, of course, if they are old pots and may be infected by diseases from plants grown in them previously. With new clay pots, the plan is to soak them overnight in cold water. The concrete pots can be treated similarly, but there is no need to soak a plastic pot.

The reason that one pots loosely at this stage is so that one can pot more firmly later on. There is always a tendency for the ball of soil to 'compact' owing to watering, and therefore when 'potting on', the soil which is put around the 3-inch pot ball must be rammed, or otherwise when watering, this ball will not be moistened because the water will flow down the looser compost on the outside. Therefore, start with loose potting, and if you have to pot on twice, on each occasion the new compost used around the original ball must be firm.

Once all the pot plants are in their 3-inch pots these may either be stood pot thick on the staging of a cool house, or if preferred they may go out into a heated frame. At this juncture the temperature does not need to be any more than about 50 deg. F., the idea being to keep out the frost and to ensure that the plants are growing slowly. Some gardeners stand them on the staging of the greenhouse for ten to fourteen days and then when they know that rooting has taken place satisfactorily, they get the plants out into cold frames, standing them so that the leaves are just not touching one another.

It is impossible to leave chrysanthemums at this stage to look after themselves (or at any other stage, for that matter!). As they grow, for instance, the plan is to space the pots out a little more. They should start to get bushy as the side growths develop, and by about a week before they are to be potted on into the 5-inch pots they ought to be spaced out to about this distance, i.e. 5 inches. All the time that they are growing in frames no coddling must be attempted. Remember the time is coming when they are going to grow out-of-doors with all the winds of heaven blowing on them, and so they need to be really hardy from the start.

This means that it is always necessary to give plenty of ventilation. The conditions must be cool. The night temperature should be about 38 deg. F. and no more, but of course it may rise owing to sun heat in the day. Avoid draughts, however, at all costs. It is better on the whole to remove a whole light than to lift up corners at one end and the other and so allow a miniature howling gale to pass through. Take care, however, not to allow the plants to be damaged by frost. Always be prepared to cover down with the glass when the temperature drops, and it may be necessary during frosty periods, especially at night time, to cover the frames with rolls of hessian, old sacks and the like. Some gardeners use straw for this purpose which they compost later.

The first potting on

The plants have been growing well in their 3-inch pots. They have been watered when necessary, that is to say, only when the plants really needed it. The compost was properly made up to the John Innes formula so that the plants had enough food, and now comes the first move. This must

take place long before the roots start to wind around the
outside of the pot and become matted. Pot on, therefore,
always before over rooting. It differs from year to year, but
generally speaking the bulk of the first potting on will be
done during the third or fourth week of March. This time
the J.I.P. Compost No. 3 is used. Look over the plants
carefully as the work proceeds, and if there is any sign of
a black or green aphis attacking the plants dip them in a
bucket of water containing nicotine and a spreader (for-
mula: $\frac{1}{4}$ ounce of nicotine to a $2\frac{1}{2}$-gallon bucketful of water,
plus 4 ounces of Shellestol).

As the plants are turned out of their 3-inch pots remove
the crock and release the roots a little. Place sufficient of the
compost in the bottom of the new pot so that it fills it about
half way, then stand the ball of soil in the centre and take
up the new compost in the right hand while holding the
plant in position with the left. Pour the compost out of the
hand around the outside of the ball of soil and firm with
a 6-inch long stick about an inch in diameter, slightly
tapered at the base, which is called a 'rammer'. Do not
ram too hard at this time because there is one more potting
on to do and the soil will need to be firmer on the last
occasion.

When the plant has been potted up, not only should there
be the new compost underneath the plant and on the two
sides, but there should be about half an inch covering the
top of the ball of soil. Further, the final soil level should be
1 inch from the rim of the pot. Never bury the plant in
the new compost, or root rotting may take place. See this
time that there are several crocks at the base of the 5-inch
pots and on top of the crocks a little rough turfy material
or a $\frac{1}{2}$-inch layer of horticultural peat.

The pots when ready can go back to the cold frames,
where they can stand close together rim to rim. Put the

lights over them for three or four days so as to help them to recover properly from this potting-on operation, and at the end of this period it should be possible to remove the glass lights altogether. It should not be necessary to water heavily, because the compost used should be in the right condition, that is to say, just moist, i.e. not so wet that when squeezed any moisture oozes out and yet not so dry that the handful of soil falls to pieces when the hand is opened after the squeezing. It should retain its shape and is then in the correct condition.

The first stopping or timing

The plants should be growing quite happily in their 5-inch pots in the comparative shelter of the frame, and about the end of April it will probably be necessary to pinch out the growing points of the plants which are to be flowered on their second crowns and thus ensure the right number of branches. They will probably by this time have produced about three or four little 'breaks' already. Some, of course, find it impossible to find enough frames for the plants at this stage, and so they stand them out on a good thick ash bed in a sheltered place. It is possible to provide temporary shelter from winds by erecting hessian or sacking on posts and wires about 4 feet high. Another alternative is to use baled straw. These bales are laid one upon the other to a height of 4 or 5 feet, and give ideal protection, say on the north and east sides. The straw is not wasted, because it is used for composting later.

The second potting on

As the plants have been grown on quietly and have been provided with the right food and protection, it should be possible to pot them up into their final pots during the second week of May. Most varieties will grow satisfactorily in 8-inch pots, but the stronger growing kinds will like to be in those that are 10-inch. Some gardeners insist on using 9-inch pots right the way through – they say this serves for all varieties and makes for standardisation. Not a bad idea! The J.I.P. Compost No. 4 must be used, and as has already been suggested, very firm potting is necessary at this stage. The great advantage of using the J.I.P. No. 4 is that even though it is well rammed into position it never impedes the passage of either air or water. Do not over-crock; just use one large piece of broken pot over the hole and do not put any peat or other rough stuff over the top.

Once again, fill the pot up about halfway with the new compost when rammed hard. Stand the ball of soil on top, having removed the crock first, and see to it that the top of this ball is about 2 inches from the top of the rim of the pot. This will allow plenty of the new compost to be rammed in all round and ensure that there is a $\frac{1}{2}$ inch of compost over the top. Thus when the potting is completed, the new level of the soil will be $1\frac{1}{2}$ inches below the rim of the pot. Of course, you will be using clean pots, and those that have been used before will have been soaked in boiling water as advised for the 3-inch pots, on page 86.

The standing ground

It is necessary to provide a *sheltered* level site on which the chrysanthemum pots can be stood. (That is the reason growers often provide wind breaks, see photograph, page 45.) The site should be covered at least 1 inch deep – and preferably 2 inches deep – with clinkers that have been crushed fairly finely. It is most important to prevent there being any rooting through the bottom of the pots into the soil below, and it is equally important to prevent worms from working up from the soil below into the pots. If there are plenty of good rough ashes and these are level and rolled down hard, there is little trouble with weeds either – and that is an important point.

It is convenient to stand the pots on to this ashed ground in a series of double rows. These rows are best arranged so as to run north and south. The pots in the two rows may be allowed to touch one another, but those who are growing for show like to stand the pots so that they are 10 or 12 inches away from their neighbours. Few of us, however, have a big enough standing ground for this purpose. The plan then is to have a double row of pots standing next to one another and then a 3-feet path in between, another two rows of pots, another 3-feet path, and so on. Once again, those who exhibit often allow a 4-feet path.

Posts, ties and bamboos

It is important, of course, to provide bamboos or thin stakes to which the plants can be tied. Before the war some of us used to use galvanised rods, because these were clean and did not harbour red spiders, and lasted for ever. The day of galvanised rods may come again! The canes should be 5 feet long, and one must be pushed carefully into each pot as close to the base of the plant as possible. Some writers have said that the bamboos ought to be pushed in without damaging the roots, but to be able to do this after potting up would be a miracle!

The plan now is to provide a stout post driven in the ground at the end of each double row. A strong wooden T-piece should then be nailed on to each post at about 4 feet 6 inches from ground level and wires should be stretched tightly from either end of one of the T's and be attached firmly to the ends of the other T so that the wires run parallel to the pots below. If these wires are really taut, it is then possible to tie the canes to the wires and thus provide the right kind of protection from high winds. If such wires are not provided, the pots will undoubtedly blow over during the first gale.

The plants themselves will be tied to the canes by means of three-ply fillis, or raffia. Remember that the tie must be sufficiently loose around the plant to allow for swelling, and then as the chrysanthemum grows further ties will be made as and when necessary. Some growers aim to give a tie every 6 inches, and others every 8 inches. Occasionally, gardeners use three canes per pot, pushed in at an angle of about 45 degrees so as to produce what may be called an inverted tripod. It is then only possible to tie two of these canes to the wires and to leave the third one sticking out. The advantage of this system is that the plants can be allowed to grow more naturally and never have that awkward bunched-up appearance as when the tying in is done to a single stake. However, this three-bamboo method entails far more work and is more expensive and so few people adopt it today.

There are naturally all kinds of alternatives to the post-and-wire method described above. It is possible, for instance, to use angle irons and then to bolt on the T-pieces. Some experts have devised an aluminium post with a T-piece that is screwed on into position with a nut and butterfly bolt. This allows the T-piece to be raised 6 inches or so in the case of the taller varieties which may need 6-feet bamboos, or may be lowered in the case of varieties like Loveliness that never grow much higher than 4 feet and so only need a 4-feet cane. The great thing is to use strong posts with wires that are stretched really tightly and thus to be able to support the weight of the pots in any strong wind.

Stopping the second time

It will be remembered that the plants that are to flower

on the second crown buds were stopped towards the end of April, and a second stopping will have to take place, therefore, about the second or third week of June. This practice is necessary for the majority of the December-flowering varieties. Friendly Rival being the well-known exception that proves the rule. However, the Stopping Tables which are given on pages 53–68 do provide a true picture of what should happen in an average year. By the time of this second stopping about four good laterals should have developed, and in fact it is better to rub off any weaker or minor breaks that develop below these. The idea is to try to get the plants to produce ten to twelve good flowering shoots from now on.

In the case of the November-flowering varieties only one stopping will be necessary as a rule, and this will take place late in May or early in June. As I have explained in Chapter VII, it undoubtedly pays to stop most of the late varieties twice, for not only can the flowering shoots be doubled and the stems made sturdier, but in addition better flowers are produced. It is possible, of course, to stop batches of plants at different dates with, say, a week in between with the idea of prolonging the flowering period of any particular variety, and readers may like to experiment along these lines.

Watering and feeding

When the plants are first stood out on the ashes there should be no need to water for about ten days, for the John Innes Compost should contain sufficient moisture to keep the plant going for that period. It is, however, important never to allow the compost to shrink in the pots and so to leave a little space between the pot wall and the big ball of soil. It may therefore be necessary to water at the end of a week if there is any shrinkage tendency at all. From that point onwards watering will have to be done about once a week, and on each occasion a good soaking will be given. There is nothing wrong in watering the pots by means of a hose providing there is a good big rose at the end which will prevent a jet of water from washing compost out of the pot.

The trouble about watering, of course, is that some plants may need a good deal of water and some hardly any or none at all. It makes a lot of difference if one man has done the potting. In that case there will be a much more even demand for water throughout the whole batch, because each ball of soil will tend to be of the same firmness. It is often when a number of people are concerned with potting that some plants are firmer in the compost than others, and then variations in the demands for water may occur. Varieties with more leaves or bigger foliage naturally tend to demand more water than smaller plants or those with less foliage. It is therefore necessary to treat each pot as an individual rather than to splash the water about any old how.

I have found out from experience, that it is usually after the third or fourth watering that the plants start to settle down as regards their demands. In the earlier stages there may be quite great differences, but after the fourth watering almost all plants of the same variety will need the same amount. The season starts with watering once a week, and by about midsummer when the weather is really hot it may be necessary to water every two days or even twice a day. Watering can be a tedious job, but it is the kind of work to do early in the morning and/or early in the evening using a nice length of hose plus the special copper 'roses' which slip easily on to the end of the hose. These are made and can be bought especially for the purpose.

Hints on feeding have been given fairly freely in Chapter VI. The special notes here are that liquid feeding must

commence the moment the bulk of the roots have pene-
trated right through the new compost placed in the large
pots. Some gardeners turn out one typical plant carefully
so as to make certain that they know when feeding time
has arrived. The danger is that beginners feed too late, and
if one had to advise a rule-of-thumb method it would be
that the plants should start to be fed ten days after the June
stop. Most growers like to feed once every ten days right
up to the time of flowering, and it certainly is necessary to
go on feeding even after the plants have been put into the
greenhouse where they are to flower. For further instructions, follow the directions given in Chapter VI.

Hand-weeding and tying in

One of the more 'honorous' jobs that must be done is to
hand-weed the soil in the pots. No weeds must ever be
allowed to develop which will compete with the chrysanthemums. It is convenient to go down the rows with a
bucket and to pop the weeds into this so that they can be
carried away and thrown on to the compost heap to rot
down as manure. Weeds not only rob the plants but they
also provide a breeding ground for pests and diseases.

Tie in the side growths as they develop by putting a
double twist around the bamboo and then one loose tie
around the stem. Unfortunately it is necessary to go over
the plants once a week for this work so as to make certain
that all laterals receive their ties when they are about 4 or
5 inches long. During the tying operation any side shoots
not required may be removed. The tyer must keep a look-
out for pests and diseases and take the necessary means of
control if and when these are seen.

During the weeding or tying keep a sharp look-out for
the suckers, or basal growths as these are called, which
grow up from the roots or from the bottoms of the stems.

Cut these off just below soil level with the sharp blade of a knife the moment they are seen. The same knife can be used for removing the unwanted laterals because, remember, the aim is to produce about ten or twelve good branches and no more.

Housing the pots

It should be possible to have secured the buds of the varieties which are to flower in November by about September 15th (see page 58). On the other hand, it is seldom that the buds of the December-flowering kinds are secured until after the pots have been brought into the greenhouse. The date of this housing actually differs from district to district and from county to county. Normally speaking, however, the aim in the North is to get the plants in under cover by September 25th and in the South some time in October. Frosts may occur at any time after these dates.

Take great care when carrying the plants in from the standing ground to the greenhouse. It pays to use a flat-bottomed truck with pneumatic tyres for the purpose; not only is the work done more expeditiously, but there is less likelihood of damage taking place. Most experts seem to advise that the plants should be given a really good watering just prior to housing, but at the Horticultural Training Centre we have discovered that it pays to omit the watering for three or four days beforehand so that when the plants are moved the leaves are flaccid and 'droopy' and so do not break off so easily as they do when they are turgid and stiff.

The ground in the greenhouses must be absolutely level and, of course, free from any debris. In the very tall houses it is possible to stand the plants on staging, and in fact in conservatories tiered staging is provided specially for the

Disbudding late-flowering chrysanthemums. Note method of staking for protection against wind damage. The tops of the bamboos are tied to the wires running from the crossbars.

A good variety to grow is the bright yellow, called Imperial Yellow.

purpose. In the normal way, however, the pots are stood on the ground so as to allow them about 12 inches of 'breathing space' on all sides. Some definite arrangement must be planned so as to make it possible to get at the pots for watering. Most growers believe in setting them out three rows to a bed running the length of the house and then they leave a 21- or 24-inch wide pathway between the three rows and the next three rows. This scheme is useful in the case of long commercial houses. In the smaller houses of amateurs it is just sufficient to arrange the pots so that they are 18 inches from one another on what is called the diagonal or zig-zag basis.

It does pay to give the plants a thorough spraying with a colloidal sulphur wash such as Bouisol about four days before housing, with the idea of preventing a serious attack of mildew. It is important to keep the temperature of the house quite cool after the chrysanthemums are in, though if it should be raining or the atmosphere be very humid a little heat will be necessary to keep the air in the house buoyant.

If the temperature is round about 50 degrees at night time and is allowed to rise a little during the day owing to sun heat, all should be well. Never coddle; always fling the ventilators wide open and only close down when the thermometer or the 'weather signs' show that there is going to be a good frost. Aim to have a free circulation of air, keep the temperature as constant as possible, and do not forget to go on watering and feeding as advised on pages 93–95. Later on, if it is desired to hurry the plants on a little, the temperature, of course, may be allowed to rise, but always ventilate as much as you possibly can or there is bound to be trouble from mildew and perhaps rust.

Once the plants are in the greenhouse it will of course be possible to control pests and to a certain extent diseases,

G

by fumigation and Aerosol methods, details of which will be found in Chapter XVI. It will not be long before the buds will be secured, and then disbudding will take place so as to ensure that one really good bloom is produced at the head of each lateral.

Varieties

A fairly complete list of varieties with their descriptions will be found in Chapter XIV. All that I am attempting to do here is to select a few of the kinds I find do best, giving their colours and approximate flowering dates.

NOVEMBER FLOWERING

Variety	Description
Apricot Loveliness	A beautiful apricot type of Loveliness whose flowers have a flat look.
Apricot May Wallace	An apricot-coloured sport of May Wallace, usually flowers a little later.
Balcombe Flame	A lovely orange-red reflexed petals.
Bronze Ace	A beautiful incurved bronze, tall. Poor lateral producer.
Cheshunt White	Reflexed pure white blooms. End November.
Crensa	A cerise tipped with buff.
Dawn Light	A reflexed beautiful cerise. Flowers November on first crown buds.
Enid Goffe	Brilliant crimson, large, first class.
Fiona	Bronze with gold tips, flattish blooms.
Golden Ace	Beautiful golden sport of Bronze Ace.
Ivory Queen	Good shaped flowers, creamy white.
Lilac Loveliness	A lilac mauve sport of Loveliness.
Loveliness	A beautiful silvery lilac, flowers rather flat.
May Wallace	One of the best pinks, blooms large and flat.
Mrs Ross	A pure white incurved.
Rose Chochod	A deep pink slightly mauve, old but good.
Yellow Ace	Another good sport of Bronze Ace.
Yellow Fiona	An excellent yellow sport of Fiona.
Yellow Orb	An incurved rich yellow, lasts well in water.

DECEMBER FLOWERING

Variety	Description
Agnes Ford	Old rose with golden reverse, reflexed. Late December.
Amber Favourite	A grand amber sport of The Favourite.
American Beauty	A white incurved, produces few cuttings, leaves rather pale.
Baldock's Crimson	A good old favourite, strong, flowers crimson-scarlet, reflexed.
Barbara Green	Often confused with Friendly Rival, but less subject to the rust disease.
Dawn Light	A reflexed cerise, flowers at Christmas on second crown buds.
Favourite	A very popular white, usually mid-December but with care can be made to stay the course till late December.
Favourite Supreme	A pinkish sport of Favourite with bronze shading.
Friendly Rival	A wonderful Christmas yellow, incurved, often badly attacked by rust.
Golden Favourite	A grand golden sport of Favourite.
January Gold	Far more bronze than gold but very late flowerer.
Late Delight	A beautiful pink Christmas flowerer, must be grown hard.
Monument	A shining white incurved.
Red Favourite	A very popular red sport of The Favourite.
Shirley Late Red	Grand for Christmas, petals rolled and deep red.
Snow	Produces flattish white blooms early in December.
Sussex Bronze	A good bronze for about the third week in December.
Western King	One of the best Christmas varieties, blooms flat and large, white.
Yellow American Beauty	An incurved bright yellow sport of American Beauty.

CHAPTER XI

Five-inch Pot Plants

DURING the last fifteen years there has been quite a move along the line of producing what may be called dwarf chrysanthemums in pots, which can be used quite happily as centre pieces for the dining-room table or just as decorative pot plants in the house. The idea is to grow the plants in 5-inch pots and to treat them in quite a different manner to the plants grown for cut bloom. After all, you are aiming to produce a plant which may be no higher than 2 feet or so, and it is only possible to do this with certain varieties, the best of which will be found listed on page 103.

The cuttings

Some people strike the cuttings during late March and April in 5-inch pots, which should contain the John Innes Potting Compost No. 1. Six cuttings are usually struck around the pot, and when these are rooted the plants are potted on into 3-inch pots, using the John Innes Potting Compost No. 1.

Others find it preferable to take stem cuttings during the months of April and May and to strike these in the usual manner in boxes as described on page 36. This late batch of cuttings fits quite happily into the normal cropping scheme of the greenhouse because the other plants are well out of the way by that time. Once the cuttings have struck they are potted up into 3-inch pots, using the J.I.P. Compost No. 1, and later on they are potted on into their 5-inch pots, using the J.I.P. Compost No. 3.

Stopping

It is usually necessary to stop twice and to aim at producing twelve good blooms on the second crown buds. With some varieties you can get quite good flowers by leaving fourteen or fifteen stems after the second stop. The great thing when pinching the plants back is to do it fairly hard, because it must be remembered that the idea is to produce sturdy bushy plants. Try and get, say, four laterals at the first stop and then at the second timing another three or four, making from twelve to sixteen in all. As to the dates of stopping, these are usually similar to the normal pot plants, that is to say about mid-April and mid-June. The difference is that rather more of the growing point of the branches is removed.

Hardening off and standing out

Treat the pots in a similar manner as advised in Chapter X for the normal pot chrysanthemums. Directly the hardening off is done, the pots may be stood out on to the ashes and remain there during the summer. It is very important to water regularly, but curiously enough, with these dwarf pot plants it is necessary in addition to syringe the leaves over thoroughly at least once a week.

It pays to space them out 15 inches apart either way so that they have got plenty of room for development and so that adequate pest and disease control may be carried out. As the plants do not grow very tall it is not always necessary to provide post-and-wire support for them, and if they are firmly placed on to the ashes they usually remain upright, especially if protection is given on the windward side of the standing ground.

Staking

With most varieties it is just sufficient to tie one single

strand of raffia right around the middle of the plant just to keep the branches together. If a gardener does experience a little trouble with branches falling or drooping, the scheme then is to split a normal bamboo into three or four, or to use a very thin cane and to push this right into the centre of the pot. It is then not difficult to put a loop round each lateral and to tie this to the central cane. It is rather a long job but it is very effective, and as the plant grows the cane and the raffia ties are hidden.

Pest and disease control

Unfortunately, plants grown in this way seem far more susceptible to pests and diseases than chrysanthemums which are allowed to grow more naturally. Aphides can be a great curse, and may be controlled by spraying with nicotine and a spreader (formula: 1 ounce of nicotine, 3 ounces of Shellestol, to 10 gallons of water). Leaf miner is also very troublesome, and measures should be taken as advised on page 174. Presumably because the plants are more bushy and so less air gets to them, mildew is the disease which can easily ruin the leaves. It always helps tremendously if the John Innes Compost has been used and if watering is properly carried out, for if there is any dryness at the roots mildew is always particularly bad. Take the precautions advised on page 165 and so make certain that this disease is kept down.

Feeding

The rules about feeding as advised on pages 49 to 51 apply largely to these dwarf pot plants. The tendency, however, must always be to keep the potash content of the feed up so that the leaves will tend to be harder and not so likely to be attacked by either pests or diseases.

Varieties

The following varieties have been grown successfully as dwarf plants in 5-inch pots. Note that some need planting one to a pot, others at two to a pot, and the majority three to a pot.

Variety	Description	No. to a pot
Blanche Poitevene	Pure white	3
Bronze Marcus	A pleasing bronze	2
Bronze Morris	One of the best known for the purpose	2
Cranfordia	Excellent yellow variety	3
Elegance	Beautiful shell pink	3
Janté Wells	Bright golden-yellow pompon	1
Jean Pattison	A lovely bronze	1
Loveliness	Very attractive silver lilac	3
Shoesmith's Yellow	A bright yellow – dark leaves	2
Sunbeam	One of the brightest yellows	3
Wendy	Lovely orange-amber	3
Yellow Morris	A good sturdy yellow	2

CHAPTER XII

Single-flowering Chrysanthemums

OVER the period of years that I have had the pleasure of taking visitors around the trial grounds, first of all of the Cheshire School of Agriculture, then of the gardens of the Swanley Horticultural College, and now the Horticultural Training Centre of which I am Principal, I have been most interested in noting people's preferences. There are some who go for the single chrysanthemum every time. They cannot understand why gardeners must grow the big double blooms. They much prefer what they call the charming, dainty, light type of flower that the single kinds produce.

Some visitors, on the other hand, curiously enough are very surprised to find that there are single varieties at all. They imagine, for some reason or another, that all chrysanthemums are double, and they place the singles into the category of the *Chrysanthemum maximum* or ox-eye daisy. There are, of course, many varieties of *Chrysanthemum maximum* grown for market, and sometimes these are treated with a dye and as a result the petals may be bronze, yellow, red, and even blue. These dyed 'monstrosities', as they have been called, undoubtedly sell well and have a similar appearance, of course, to many of the single kinds of pyrethrum.

Anyway, it is only obvious that in a book of this sort one must give a fair place to the single varieties of chrysanthemum, because there must be readers who much prefer them to the doubles.

As far as culture is concerned, this does not differ from the normal methods as described, for instance, in Chapter

VIII in the case of the earlies and in Chapter X in respect of the lates. It is possible to carry out a certain amount of disbudding so as to ensure that the blooms are larger, but it can be said without fear of contradiction that all singles stand wet weather better than doubles, and most are far hardier as regards frost. I can, therefore, strongly recommend singles to those who have a garden which tends to be a 'frost pocket'.

The November and December singles

The November and December singles are no more difficult to grow than any of the double varieties, and in fact I would say they are easier. The plants may break naturally during the first two weeks of May. Go over the plants, however, and if any should not be breaking as they should by say, May 18th, stop them. There is, perhaps, one exception to this rule, and that is the terra-cotta variety Desert Song. This needs 'timing' at the end of April.

It should be possible to secure the buds of the majority of the singles before the end of the second week of September. It is when the flowering buds appear before this that there is always a danger that some doubling occurs. If one is growing singles, of course, the great aim is to produce perfect examples of the type, and any kind of 'doubling up' is of course frowned upon.

Varieties of late-flowering singles

The author is particularly fond of late-flowering singles, and below will be found a list of varieties which he recommends.

Variety	Description
Artist	One of the brightest rich crimsons with good hard petals, 4 feet.
Audax	A very large pink, 4½ feet.
Betty Woolman	A lovely golden amber, 5 feet.

Variety	Description
Broadacre	A perfect white, good for exhibition, 3 feet.
Caroline	A very pleasing pink with large flowers, 4 feet.
Cleopatra	A strong growing terra-cotta bronze.
Crimson Defiance	A deep crimson on golden ground.
David Green	A large Indian red.
Deborah	An excellent bright pink, good for exhibition, 4 feet.
Desert Chief	A fawn terra-cotta with gold tips, $3\frac{1}{2}$ feet.
Desert Moon	A lovely yellow.
Doris Bloor	A terra-cotta with salmon suffusion.
Dorothy Thomas	Probably the best pure white grown, 4 feet.
Evelyn Ogg	A brilliant red with golden reverse.
Golden Seal	Perhaps the most popular deep yellow, 4 feet.
Hussar	Strong grower, mid crimson, large flowers.
Josephine Wells	A glowing purple, quite a distinct colour.
Lilian Jackson	A rose with a white disc, dwarf habit, 3 feet.
Mary Lee	A fine large rich pink, 4 feet.
Mary Siddon	A large flowered crimson, excellent for exhibition.
Mason's Bronze	A terra-cotta bronze, one of the most popular, $4\frac{1}{2}$ feet.
Orange Glory	An orange on golden ground, a glorious colour, $4\frac{1}{2}$ feet.
Peter Robinson	One of the largest yellows, good for exhibition, 5 feet.
Phyllis Cooper	A rich golden yellow, medium flowers.
Pretty	A delightful shade of pink with a distinct white disc, 4 feet.
Rob Roy	A crimson red with a yellow ring, 4 feet.
Rubens	A deep rosy carmine, good for exhibition, $4\frac{1}{2}$ feet.
Sabu	A rich rose, overlaid with bronze, always very popular, $4\frac{1}{2}$ feet.
Satan	A dark crimson, free flowerer.
Susan	A grand rosy bronze, on yellow ground, 5 feet.
Torch	A yellow, deepening to orange and suffused with salmon at the tips.

The early-flowering singles

In the earlier part of the chapter I have made it quite clear that there is no more difficulty in growing single varieties than doubles – in fact, on the whole, I think singles are easier to grow. They are not so easily damaged by the weather; double flowers are often spotted by the rain or damaged by the wind, whereas in the case of singles the rain drops seem to fall off the petals more easily, and the flowers being more dainty do not provide such a resistance to wind.

There is nothing special to say, therefore, about their cultivation. They can be planted, manured and looked after in exactly the same way as the ordinary early-flowering chrysanthemums mentioned in Chapter VIII.

Varieties of early-flowering singles

Variety	Description
Afton	Free flowering bright pink, early September.
Columbine	A rose strawberry, long stems, September.
Curlew	A bright rose, long sprays, August.
Dainty	Deep yellow, excellent, September.
Donald Wells	A pure white, long stems, August.
Doreen Woolvern	Bright orange, erect grower, early September.
Early Mary Richardson	Buff shaded, golden amber. A shapely bush, late September.
Edith	Lovely rose pink, good disbudder.
Elaine	A large spreading bush with pink flowers, 3 feet.
Firebrand	A terra-cotta red, spindly grower, August.
Fire King	Bright crimson red, August.
Gillian	A vivid crimson scarlet, September.
Golden Firebrand	A bright yellow, similar to Firebrand.
Golden Gleam	A bright orange, July, gives semi-double flowers to start with which turn to single when the blooms are older.
Jean	A soft rosy bronze with a nice light zone, September.

Variety	*Description*
Keith	A yellow which produces a mass of flowers, 2½ feet, September.
Kitty	One of the largest singles when disbudded. A rose with a large white zone, August.
Lance	A bright crimson, upright grower, August.
Maidenhood	A pale primrose, strong grower, large flowers when disbudded, early September. If left for spray, early October.
Nectar	A free-blooming almond blossom pink, September.
Peerless	A charming golden yellow, mid-September.
Red Letter	Bright scarlet, large flowers with slightly incurved florets, mid-September.
Red Riding Hood	A beautiful red with large flowers which are held out stiffly, early September.
Richard Holding	Brilliant chestnut scarlet with yellow centre, early September.
Shirley Crimson	A deep rich crimson with golden yellow disc, rather dark, early September.
Shirley Terra-cotta	A bright terra-cotta with firm fine flowers, heavy cropper, mid-September. Excellent in artificial light.
Snowstorm	A pure white with greenish centre, 2 feet, September.
Valerie	A beautiful rose pink, good grower, flowers August onwards.
Vicar of Shirley	A rich deep bronze, good grower, erect habit, mid-September.
Waterwitch	A dwarf-growing pure white, flowers mid-September until a serious frost, 2 feet.

CHAPTER XIII

The Exhibitor and Exhibiting

IT is only natural that those who are keen on chrysanthemums should like to enter some of their blooms in the various classes at the local shows. Very often success at a local show encourages a man or woman to go on to greater heights and to compete at the national show. I cannot do better at this stage than to recommend all readers to join the National Chrysanthemum Society,* because not only is there much to be learned from the big shows the Society is able to organise, but there is great help to be got from the Year Books which are issued every twelve months.

The prospective exhibitor must, of course, take far more care of his blooms than the man who is just growing to satisfy the needs of his own house. The marks made by earwigs for instance, in a single night, may not unduly depress a home producer, but to the exhibitor they may make all the difference between a Silver Cup and no prize at all. The greatest of care, therefore, has to be taken to follow out the instructions given in Chapter XVI, and sometimes the use of insecticides has to be followed by actual hand picking of pests.

The beginner often goes for size and for size only, but too often the immense blooms are coarse and perhaps stale. The judge therefore prefers a more moderate-sized bloom which is perfect in shape and colour and which looks absolutely fresh. It is far better to have, for instance, a

---

* The National Chrysanthemum Society (Secretary: E. T. Thistlethwaite), 83 Chesterfield Road, Barnet, Herts.

chrysanthemum flower which is just coming to perfection than one which was perfect a few days ago and by the time it is put on the show bench is just going downhill.

Remember that the judge looks everywhere. He will look in the middle of a bloom to see whether, in the case of doubles, there is any sign at all of the eye; he will look underneath the blooms to try to discover whether there are any old petals which are past their best; and the successful exhibitor will remove these carefully with, maybe, a pair of forceps. Many cut their flowers four days previous to the show if they are in the right condition, and they then put them in water in a cool place so that they come to the show looking absolutely fresh. If possible, however, leave the blooms on the plants until two days before they are needed, and in the case of varieties which do not take water up easily, after cutting crush the ends of the stems with a pair of pliers so as to make sure that the water can rise. Some experts say that a little salt in the water helps, using about a teaspoonful to a pint and a half of water.

When putting the stems into water it is necessary to remove some of the bottom leaves, or else these may absorb much of the moisture, which will not, as a result, get right up to the flower. See that the atmosphere in the room is quite dry and that the light is partially excluded. If the blooms are kept dry in this way it is an easier matter to remove any of the damaged florets. It is always a good plan to cut more flowers than are actually needed for the exhibit so that the choice of the final six, eight or twelve blooms, or whatever it may be, can be made from a fairly wide selection.

If six blooms are needed of a particular variety, the colours of these flowers must be absolutely uniform. They should be of the same size and of the same shape. The stems should be of the same length, and, in fact, the more identical they can be the better. This means that it is important to cut all the blooms which are to be shown in one class on one day, because fortunately, or unfortunately, an expert judge can easily detect, by the loss of sheen, blooms which have been cut a day or two before others.

Read the schedule

As one who has judged at a large number of shows, I would urge that the schedules be read very carefully. It is surprising how often exhibits have to be disqualified in local shows because where six flowers have been asked for, five have been entered, or even seven. Read the schedule, and if you do not understand its implication go to some local expert and he will be delighted to explain the whole thing to you. For instance, when a schedule asks for 'Decorative Chrysanthemums' you are expected to enter decoratives and not any other type. If, on the other hand, the particular class says twelve blooms of any variety or varieties it has been discovered that judges usually give higher points to a vase which contains twelve identical blooms of one definite kind than to a similar vase which contains flowers of different varieties – remember, of course, that singles are not doubles (though even here there has been confusion in the past) and do not forget that rayonnantes are not decoratives. It never hurts to ask questions from a committee member before the show, for it can be very hurtful to be disqualified.

It is a very good plan to go round the show the year before in order to make notes of the varieties that have won in each class, the size of the blooms, the length of the stem, and so on. It is surprising what can be learnt from other exhibitors, especially if a particular winning entry is admired and the one who has been successful is there at the time. He can often be persuaded to give advice there and then.

Notice how the blooms have been staged. Find out whether you have to provide your own vases or whether the society loans them to all who enter the competition. In cases where it is necessary to provide the flower-containers see that these are of the right size and shape. Buy them well in advance, for at the time of writing good vases are not easy to get.

At the show itself

The blooms have been chosen; they have been very carefully packed in deep boxes so that they cannot move about; special pads made of wood wool with paper around them have been provided on which the necks of the blooms can rest. The result is that the chrysanthemums will arrive at the show undamaged. Get there as early as you can so as to have plenty of time for staging. The committee will tell you the time you may arrive. Convey the boxes to the show carefully, and when they arrive there, do not leave the boxes out in the sun or rain, but get them in the cool under cover.

You will find that it will do you no harm to give a helping hand to another exhibitor by helping him carry in his boxes or by assisting in some other way. Friendliness among exhibitors is a good thing and must be encouraged. See that the vases have plenty of water in them and then start to arrange the chrysanthemums in accordance with the needs of the schedule and in order that the flowers may look at their best when the judges come round an hour or two later. Do not spend the time watching other exhibitors. Get on with your own work. If any of the blooms have unfortunately had any dust fall on them during the journey, remove this very carefully with a camel-hair brush. If any of the florets are out of place, it is often possible to re-arrange them with a pair of forceps.

GOLDEN SCEPTRE

Though it is extremely important to give yourself plenty of time for arranging the blooms, it is not advantageous to expose the exhibits too long before the actual judging, and some therefore cover up the flowers with a little tissue paper to protect them until they are called out of the tent or room for the actual judging. Be sure that the right card is put at the base of the vase or vases. Take care that the right blooms are entered in the right class. It is quite possible to get confused if one class asks for three white decoratives and another for five white decoratives. Many a man in entering both classes has put the three-bloom vase in the five-bloom class.

This leads me on to say that when starting to show it is always better to concentrate on one or two classes and to go for these with great fervour. It is very easy to dissipate one's strength by trying to enter too many classes in one season. It has been said that the judge goes for the five S's, i.e. Solidity, Symmetry, Substance, Smoothness, and Size, but he undoubtedly also goes for the three F's as well – Freshness, Floret colour, and Finish. Never think that size is all-important just for size's sake.

Once the flowers have been staged and the judges are doing their work my advice to all exhibitors is to leave the show and only come back again when all the judging has been completed. It is very nerve racking to stand about at the entrance to the hall or marquee; judges do not appreciate the impatience of exhibitors, and furthermore, though often an exhibitor may have a steward friend who can come and advise him, perhaps early on, of wins – even this may have its disappointments for, because of the frailty of human nature, even a steward may make a mistake in reporting to a friend.

H

Special notes on different classes

It will be as well to provide some special notes on the main classes in the show: (*a*) the early flowering, (*b*) the singles, (*c*) the medium exhibition varieties, and (*d*) the large exhibition chrysanthemums often called the Japanese chrysanthemums in the past.

The general rules about chrysanthemum growing apply naturally to the exhibition blooms as much as to those which are just to be grown for beautifying the house or garden, and it only remains to give special hints and tips which may help to make all the difference between winning a third or a first prize.

Exhibiting early-flowering varieties

Take the greatest of pains to choose the best cuttings. Take the precaution of dipping these in a nicotine solution before striking them. Rooting should have taken place within five weeks, and the plants should then be potted up into soil blocks* or 3-inch pots. The greatest of care must be taken of the roots at all stages, and if the plants can be kept in a closed frame for three days after this and be sprayed lightly each morning with clean water, quick root action will be encouraged. Shade the frame if sunny, and do not spray with water if it is frosty.

Prepare the outside bed a month before planting, adding the base organic fertiliser at the same time: a fish manure with a 5 per cent potash content is good. Water the pots or soil blocks the night before planting, and if it should be dry at planting time fill the holes with water and allow this to drain away before the ball of soil is put in. A good dusting afterwards with D.D.T. helps to keep away most pests for two or three weeks.

---

* *These are blocks of soil made by the gardener with special Soil Blocking Machines which can be bought for the purpose.*

Stop the plants in accordance with the instructions given in Chapter VII; only in the North slightly earlier stopping dates may be necessary. Aim to take from four to six breaks only, four if the variety tends to be weak, six if it is strong, and as a result you should get good blooms. When disbudding, leave all side buds until they are $\frac{1}{4}$ inch long before breaking them off, especially those around the main bud which you are going to secure. It is possible, of course, to retard flowering by pinching out the end centre bud, allowing the growth next below it to develop instead. Only experience will enable exhibitors to time their plants perfectly, but this scheme will set back the flowering dates anything from seven days to three weeks.

Some of the pink, bronze, and red shades will be spoiled as far as colour is concerned if they are given any protection at all. On the other hand, the whites and yellows may need a butter muslin length held over them for a week or two before the show. Northern growers often use dutch lights as umbrellas or parasols for a similar reason. Sometimes a little 'Summer Cloud' sprayed over the lights will prevent sun scorch. It is said that the greatest trouble is caused by the sun shining on the damp petals.

It always pays to flood the ground with water the night before cutting the blooms. Sever the stems as early in the morning as possible and having bruised the base of them, put them into a deep bucket for at least twelve hours before packing. Be sure that white blooms are white, and it helps after cutting sometimes to spray the flowers with plenty of clean water and then carefully to shake the excess water off afterwards.

Exhibiting the singles

At most shows there are very popular classes for singles, and especially the November-flowering kinds. In the case of the early-flowering singles, see the previous notes. It seems to pay with November singles to get the cuttings struck early so that it can be ensured that they are potted on into their 5-inch pots by the first week of March. Use the John Innes Potting Compost No. 2 at this stage. Do not pot too firmly, and do not water the plants in. It seems that the spraying over of the foliage is far better at this stage. Get the plants into frames and gradually harden them off.

About ten days after the first potting pinch out the growing points and so do the first stop. Only allow two breaks to develop. At the end of May pot on into 8-inch pots, using the J.I. Compost No. 3. Be sure to use plenty of crocks so that the drainage is perfect. Do a little ramming around the outside of the ball of soil so as to make certain that the new compost is of the same firmness as the old. Do not water for five days after potting, and keep the plants fresh by spraying them overhead and, if possible, standing them in a shady spot. After a week the plants can be stood on the standing ground (see page 90), the tops of the canes being tied to the wires.

The stronger varieties will have their second stopping during the first week of June and the weaker and medium-flowered varieties about the third week. This time three breaks should be allowed on each stem, and so six good blooms will be produced per plant. From mid-July onwards feed every fortnight with Liquinure (Flower Special), or every three weeks with the compounded Humber Fish Manure mixed with a little sterilised soil. This should be watered in. Never over-water. It is when the soil is over-moist that the wood can never ripen properly.

It ought to be possible to see the flowering buds at the tips of the branches about the end of August or beginning of September, and then the side buds should be removed. By the end of the second week of September all the buds should have been 'secured'. A week later the plants can go into the greenhouse where they are to flower. Feeding will then continue once every fourteen days until the flowers are half open. Give a little heat, say 55 to 60 deg. F., so as to maintain a buoyant atmosphere and prevent mildew.

The grower of singles aims to show an absolutely flat flower. Florets which are slightly incurving are not liked by judges. Some of the varieties are very tall, just about 6 feet, and therefore you want a tall greenhouse to accommodate them. All the Molly Godfrey group come into this category, i.e. Red Molly, Bronze Molly, Rose Molly, and so on. They are all very good show varieties however. Other kinds which have won prizes at shows are Rob Roy, a crimson; Jinx, a pure white; Audax, a pink; and G. H. Smart, a yellow; all these grow only 4 to 5 feet tall.

Exhibiting the medium exhibition varieties

It is not every show that has its class for medium exhibition varieties: varieties like Golden Elizabeth and Elegance. It is possible to get from four to six good flowers per plant, and most varieties are sturdy with good foliage. Take the cuttings about mid-January; get them into soil blocks or 3-inch pots the moment they have rooted, using the John Innes Potting Compost No. 1. Pot them on into the 5-inch pots by the end of March, using the John Innes Potting Compost No. 3. Be careful with the water immediately after potting, but be generous with the syringing over with clean water. It always pays to keep free from pests varieties that are to be grown for exhibition. Spraying with nicotine (formula: 1 ounce to 10 gallons of water plus 3 ounces of Shellestol) gives excellent results. Some exhibitors spray once a fortnight until the blooms start to show colour.

Get the plants into their flowering pots, either 8- or 10-inch, by the last week of May, using the John Innes

Potting Compost No. 3. Pot fairly firmly, and if the ball of soil shows any sign of dryness soak it in a bucket of water for half an hour or so before the potting-on operation takes place. Commence to feed when the roots grow through to the inside of the plants. Feed as advised for singles. House at the end of September. Never overcrowd. Use just a little heat so as to keep the air moving and the plants will not get mildew badly. Water regularly as the plants need it, but never over-water.

Exhibiting the large exhibition chrysanthemums

Get the cuttings struck as early as possible, i.e. even at the end of December. Place in a greenhouse at a temperature of 50 deg. F., and about three or four weeks later pot up into 3-inch pots, using the John Innes Potting Compost No. 1. About the third or fourth week of March pot on once more into 5-inch pots, using the John Innes Potting Compost No. 2. See that the ball of soil is thoroughly soaked before potting on. After potting, place the plants in a cold frame and keep it closed for three days. Admit air after this and gradually harden off.

Do not water for four days after potting. Keep the plants happy by spraying with water overhead. On the fifth day water heavily in the morning. Never water in the evening because this seems to encourage mildew. Spray regularly with nicotine, as advised on page 117, to control pests.

Pot on again into the 9- or 10-inch pots about the third or fourth week of May, using the John Innes Potting Compost No. 3. Use plenty of crocks to ensure good drainage. Fill the pots to within 2½ inches of the top. Place the pots on their ash beds out of doors and do not water for four days after potting. After that fill the pots almost to their rims with water through the fine rose of a can. Do this in the morning, not in the evening.

It should be possible to see the break bud during the first two weeks of June, and if this is pinched off the laterals will develop. Concentrate on the three best side growths and allow these to grow until the buds are seen at the top, when the disbudding should be carried out. The exception to the rule is in the case of a variety which is to be grown on the second crown bud. When growing these exhibition chrysanthemums it is a good plan to take advice from the nurseryman who supplies the plants, or of course you should consult Chapter VII of this book.

If three stems were allowed after the first stopping, it is usual in growing exhibition flowers to allow only one stem to develop on each branch, so that even after the second stopping there are still only three stems per plant.

Never secure the buds of exhibition varieties too early or they may go blind. As a general rule, the flowering buds may be secured any time between August 10th and 20th. The bud that is chosen then will produce a large exhibition flower for November, and most of the shows are round about that time. Do not worry, however, if the bud appears too early because the plan then is to disbud on a gradual basis, one shoot being removed this day, another two days later, another two days after that, and so on, and as a result of this gradual disbudding and dis-shooting the energy of the whole plant is not thrown into the secured bud too quickly and the flowering process is therefore delayed.

CHAPTER XIV

Varieties and their Description

THERE are, of course, a very large number of chrysanthemum varieties to choose from. It is the old, old story of 'one man's meat being another man's poison', and so, if the reader finds that the author has left out a particular name which is beloved by him or her, all that can be said is that the list is the author's choice, even though it may be an arbitrary one.

I have purposely stuck to the National Chrysanthemum Society's classified official catalogue of varieties so that those who propose to exhibit at shows will know which varieties are eligible for a particular class. Remember that the exhibitor classes the creams as whites, the primrose and orange varieties as yellows, and the crimson kinds as reds. Do not, whatever you do, try to put a bronze in a red class despite the fact that red may be part of the name of a variety. Look at the description given, and where the chrysanthemum is described as 'bronze' believe it to be bronze, even though the raiser may have unfortunately called it, for instance, Red Favourite or Red Crensa.

Where a variety is very suitable for growing un-disbudded as spray the fact has been mentioned.

I have to thank, as always, the National Chrysanthemum Society for their help in this classification.

INDOOR VARIETIES

Section I. Exhibition Incurved
  (a) Large-flowered

Variety	Description
Annie Curry	Fine large ivory-white.
Blush Curry	A pinky sport of Annie Curry.

Variety	*Description*
Buff Curry	Light buff sport from Annie Curry.
Canary Monument	Deeper yellow sport of Yellow Monument.
Captain Kettle	Golden-buff outside of petals, crimson-red centre.
Charles Hopkinson	Large yellow shaded buff flowers.
Cream Monument	Cream sport from Monument – very fine.
Godfrey's Eclipse	Rich yellow.
Golden Curry	Golden-yellow sport from Yellow Curry.
Golden Ondine	Fine golden-yellow sport from Yellow Ondine.
J. W. Cane	Large buttercup-yellow.
Lilac Monument	Good lilac-pink.
Monument	Fine white for Christmas.
Ondine	White with green tipped petals.
Percy A. Dove	Pure large white flower.
Pink Curry	Pale blush pink.
Wolverine	Old gold with inside of petals crushed strawberry.
Yellow Curry	Beautiful yellow sport from Annie Curry.
Yellow Monument	Sport of the well-known Monument.
Yellow Ondine	Citron-yellow sport from Ondine.

(b) Medium-flowered

Advancement	Sport of Progress, lovely blush-white.
Baby Royal	Deep yellow ball-like flowers.
Blazing Gold	Resembles a tight golden ball.
Bronze Progress	Very fine bronze.
Buttercup	Rich yellow.
Calypso	Fine reddish-bronze.
Clara Wells	Beautiful chrome-yellow tinged with pink.
Coronation Gold	Crimson red with gold reverse.
Golden Glory	Intense gold.
Lord Somers	Fine golden-amber.
Milton Gray	An Australian variety of creamy primrose.
Mrs H. L. Southam	Primrose sport of Progress.
Mrs J. B. Bryce	Large white tinted with rose.
Mrs P. E. Wiseman	Primrose shaded salmon.
Penrod	New yellow of great promise.
Progress	Fine silvery-pink.
Romance	Golden-yellow.
Shirley Buff	Buff shading red, wide petals.

Variety	Description
White Progress	White sport from Progress.
W. J. Hill	Deep yellow.
Yellow Progress	Good yellow sport from Progress.

Section II. *Large Exhibition* (formerly known as Japanese)

Variety	Description
A. M. Davis	Deep pink with silver reverse.
Annie Baker	Large deep rose pink with attractive silver reverse
Archie Woolman	Crimson shaded claret blooms.
Bacchante	Large crimson with gold reverse.
Ben Franklin	Very attractive pure pink.
Bert Webb	Fine deep yellow.
Birmingham	Good crimson with gold reverse.
Break O'Day	Maize yellow shading to bronze.
Bronze Birmingham	Bronze yellow sport from Birmingham.
Clara Trueman	Brilliant chestnut-bronze.
Cossack	Shining crimson.
Cream Duke	Fine cream sport from Duke of Kent.
Dida Bryant	Large ivory-white.
Donald Dearson	White at top with basal flush of rose.
Duchess of Kent	A very beautiful pink.
Duke of Kent	Very large white.
Edith Cavell	Rich chestnut with golden reverse.
Edith Woolman	One of the finest pinks.
Edna Green	Deep golden yellow.
E. F. Hawes	Ruby with buff reverse
Eva Woollard	Lemon-yellow seedling from H. E. Trueman.
F. E. Luxford	A most attractive apricot with centre of deeper colour
F. E. Morris	Rosy salmon with golden reverse.
Frank Doodson	Amber, shaded bronze.
Frank Payne	Lovely deep yellow.
Fred Harris	Very large rose purple.
Geoffrey Philippe	Crimson-lake with silvery reverse.
Golden Eagle	1951 spring introduction, very clear yellow.
Golden Trueman	Excellent golden yellow sport from Yellow Trueman.
Gwen Kelly	Pale rose with greenish tips in centre.
Henry E. Trueman	Very fine white.

Variety	Description
Henry Woolman	Reddish-crimson with gold centre.
H. G. Park	Rich rose with silver reverse.
Hon. Mrs E. H. Potts	Fine golden-amber.
Hugh Mitchell	Velvet-crimson with gold reverse.
Hyacinth	New shade of hyacinth-pink.
Jack McGlashen	Rich old rose, a sport from Turbulent.
Jaffa	Lovely 1949 variety of orange terra-cotta.
James Bryant	Chestnut-crimson.
Jessie Boardman	Clear yellow with pink tipped petals.
Jessie Habgood	A new very fine white.
J. F. Woolman	Pale pink with cream centre.
John Bryant	Red with buff reverse.
John Pockett	Fine rosy crimson.
Kathleen Pettinger	Large rose-pink with silver reverse.
Lancashire	A grand yellow.
Laura Geddes	Very beautiful pink.
Louisa Pockett	Huge white, tinged pink on late buds.
Magnolia	Most attractive magnolia pink.
Majestic	Intense golden-amber shade.
Mary Cameron	Excellent terra-cotta with golden reverse.
Mrs Percy Sudbury	Rose with silver reverse.
Neville Chamberlain	Deep yellow with orange-yellow centre.
Newcastle	Large pink with reverse of silver.
Owen Luxford	Crimson with dull gold reverse.
Pockett's Maroon	An interesting variety of Australian origin.
Portsmouth Champion	Apricot-bronze, shaded salmon, excellent new variety.
Primate	Deep rose with shining purple sheen.
Purple Prince	Rich purple with silver reverse.
Red Majestic	Fine terra-cotta sport from Majestic.
Remus	Deep rose with silver reverse.
Rev. Harold Chappel	A pleasing peach-pink flushed salmon, overlaid with buff
Robert Radcliffe	Very good pink.
R. Richardson	Bronze, gold reverse.
Shirley Amber	Large amber shade.
Shirley Chestnut	An excellent chestnut terra-cotta with gold at tips
Shirley Desire	Ivory white flushed pink.
Shirley Masterpiece	Extra large white.

Variety	*Description*
Shirley Perfection	Lovely bright pink with reverse of silver, 1950 variety.
Sir Austen Chamberlain	Crushed strawberry with sheen of silver-rose.
Themus	Rosy amaranth with lighter reverse.
Thomas W. Pockett	Pink with silver reverse.
Turbulent	Excellent rose-purple with silver reverse at tip of petals.
Versatile	Fine deep pink.
William Meadows	Light golden-chestnut with gold reverse.
Yellow Duke	A very fine delicate yellow sport of Duke of Kent
Yellow Majestic	Clear golden-yellow sport from Majestic.
Yellow Trueman	Yellow sport from H. E. Trueman.

Section III. Large Exhibition Incurving (formerly known as Incurving Japanese)

Variety	*Description*
Aladdin	Buff with old rose inside petals.
Alice	Primrose sport of Mrs H. Wells.
Aline	Golden-bronze.
Ann	Chestnut with buff reverse.
Bernea	Deep rose with silvery reverse.
Bertram F. Jones	Amber shaded gold.
Candeur	Pure white.
Comrade	Maize-yellow with green-tipped petals.
Coronation Buttercup	A grand gold.
D. M. Pocock	Maize tinged with apricot.
Dorothy Wyles	Very pure white tinged with pale green at base of florets.
Eric Swire	Mauve-pink with silver reverse. Good 1950 introduction.
Frances Luxford	Large mauve-pink with broad petals.
Fred Baker	Rosy purple with reverse of silver.
Fred Taylor	Very fine yellow.
Geo. Edwards	White, shaded lilac.
Gordon Habgood	Mahogany-bronze shaded gold.
Grace Burtenshaw	Light canary-yellow.
Graham Luxford	Good large yellow.

Variety	Description
Joyce Richards	Chestnut with rosy buff reverse.
Keith Luxford	1951 spring introduction of deep rose with silver reverse.
Lady Gowrie	Very large white which is easy to cultivate.
Linella	Deep rose with silver reverse.
Margaret Luxford	Blush-white when first open, when fully matured almost pure white.
Medora	Golden amber.
Mrs G. Drabble	Marble-white.
Mrs H. Habgood	Salmon shaded apricot.
Mrs H. Wells	Creamy white with green shading.
Mrs M. Sargent	White shaded green.
Mrs R. C. Pulling	Large ochre-yellow.
Primrose Candeur	Lovely primrose sport of Candeur.
Rise of Day	Apricot tinged with red, pale buff reverse.
Shirley Champion	Attractive 1950 deep yellow, the flower of which forms a ball-shape.
Shirley Primrose	Fine primrose-yellow.
Shirley Triumph	Large blush-pink.
Sybil Molyneaux	Golden sport from Yellow Candeur.
Voltaire	Crimson inside with buff reverse.
Yellow Candeur	Clear yellow sport from Candeur.

Section IV. Medium Exhibition

Variety	Description
Ada Witcher	Beautiful pearly white.
Amber Elegance	Very good amber sport from Elegance.
Annette	Pure white with broad florets.
Appert	Lovely old gold shade.
Bronze Mona Davis	Rich bronze sport of Mona Davis.
Cintra	Deep yellow well-formed flowers.
Crimson Mona Davis	Attractive crimson sport of Mona Davis.
Edward Page	Fine pure white.
Elegance	Beautiful shell pink.
Golden Mary Elizabeth	Brilliant golden sport from Mary Elizabeth.
Huntsman	Shining crimson perfectly shaped blooms.
Jane Cole	Salmon-pink sport of Mary Alesworth.
Mary Alesworth	Large pale-pink well-shaped flowers.
Mary Elizabeth	Light bronze with amber reverse.

Variety	Description
Miriam	Fine velvety-crimson with old gold reverse.
Miss Shirley Kember	Good rose-pink variety.
Mona Davis	Splendid mauve-pink.
Mrs R. Luxford	Excellent Indian-red.
Red Mary Elizabeth	Bright red sport of Mary Elizabeth.
Red Mona Davis	A red sport of Mona Davis.
Rose Elegance	Rose-pink sport of Elegance.
Rose Mona Davis	Deep rose sport of Mona Davis.
Salmon Strauss	Salmon sport of Mona Davis.
Tom Purvis	Crimson with gold reverse.
White Alesworth	Pure white sport of Mary Alesworth.
White Elegance	Good white sport of Elegance.
White Mona Davis	White sport of Mona Davis.
Winn Quinn	Good yellow variety.
Yellow Edward Page	Primrose-yellow sport of Edward Page.
Yellow Mona Davis	Lemon-yellow sport of Mona Davis.

Section V. Reflexed Decoratives

Variety	Description
Ada Stevens	Good rich golden-yellow.
Agnes Ford	Old rose with gold reverse.
Amber Late Delight	Amber-bronze sport from Late Delight.
Amber Nicolson	Bright golden-bronze sport of Mollie Nicolson.
Anona	Red with golden reverse.
Apricot Crensa	Pale apricot sport from Crensa.
Apricot Delight	Amber-bronze sport from Late Delight.
Apricot Favourite	An apricot-coloured sport of Favourite.
Apricot Loveliness	Attractive pastel-shaded sport of Loveliness.
Apricot May Wallace	Soft apricot sport from May Wallace.
Arden	Large terra-cotta blooms.
Aurora	Fine orange-bronze.
Autocrat	Very good large white.
Balcombe Flame	Brilliant flame colour.
Beverley	Very stately plants of fine golden-yellow.
Blanche Poitevene	Pure white.
Brighton Beauty	Clear pink, medium size.
Bronze Celebrity	Light bronze sport of Celebrity.
Bronze Glory	Amber-bronze, large flowers.
Bronze Late Delight	A bronzy sport of Late Delight.
Bronze May Wallace	Deep rose bronze sport from May Wallace.

Variety	*Description*
Bronze Mollie Nicolson	Golden-bronze sport from Mollie Nicolson.
Bronze Paine	Seedling from Gladys Paine of deep bronze.
Bronze Picture	Light bronze sport from Picture.
Bronze Rose	Rich bronze sport of Rose Harrison.
Celebrity	Fine golden blooms.
Cheshunt White	Synonymous to Autocrat.
Christmas Beauty	Very deep yellow.
Christmas Gold	A superb golden variety.
Christmas Red	Large rich scarlet-crimson.
Classic	A fine rich yellow.
Colham Pink	One of the best pinks in this class.
Cream Favourite	Cream sport of Favourite.
Cream Ford	Fine crimson sport from Agnes Ford.
Crensa	Lovely rosy cerise, tipped buff.
Crimson Aurora	A grand crimson.
Crimson Perfection	Rich crimson with gold reverse.
Crimson Velvet	Velvety crimson, large flowers.
Daisy Stevens	First-class pure white.
Deep Pink Favourite	Deep pink sport from Favourite.
Dora Ramsey	Large bright red.
Dorothy Jackson	Good lemon-yellow.
Dresden	Excellent porcelain-pink.
Eclipse	Attractive amber shade.
Edith Alston	Pure white.
Enfield White	Synonymous to Autocrat and Cheshunt White.
Enid Goffe	One of the best crimsons.
Enton Beauty	Rich dark velvety-crimson.
Envoy	Bright red with gold reverse.
Eventide	Pure clear pink.
Fanfare	Another good pink.
Favourite	One of the best large whites.
Favourite Supreme	Bronze-pink sport of Favourite.
Fernleigh Beauty	Bright red, strong grower.
Finale	Good orange-amber.
Fiona	Bright bronze with gold points.
Fire Glow	Fiery orange red.
Gilbert	Wonderful rosy carmine, suitable for spray.
Glacier	Very large white.
Gladys Paine	Old rose with buff reverse.

Variety	Description
Glorina	Good maize-yellow.
Golden Favourite	Similar to Yellow Favourite but of a deeper shade.
Goldilocks	A lovely blend of orange and bronze.
Harold Alston	Beautiful shining crimson.
Hassocks Beauty	Rich dark rose sport of Agnes Ford.
Heston White	Very pure white, suitable for spray.
Heston Yellow	Suitable for spray.
Imperial Pink	Brilliant rose pink.
Imperial Rose	Rich rose sport of Imperial Pink.
Ivernia	Bright shade of rich orange-red.
January Gold	Bright golden-bronze.
J. W. Morris	Rich rose pink with lighter reverse.
Late Delight	Beautiful shell-pink.
Lighthouse	A new very fine bronze.
Lilac Loveliness	Soft lilac-pink sport from Loveliness
Louie Barthou	Rich plum with silvery reverse.
Loula	Deep crimson variety with large flowers of a wonderful texture.
Loveliness	Silvery lilac, very attractive.
Magnet	Strong bright terra-cotta.
Marie Morin	A dwarf white.
Market Gold	Light amber-gold.
Market Yellow	A good yellow, firm petals.
May	New pink variety.
Mayford Purple	Rich purple with large blooms.
Mayford Rose	A lovely rose, good grower.
Mayford Salmon	Soft salmon-pink.
Mayford Success	Good rose-pink.
May Wallace	Lovely shell-pink.
Mollie Nicolson	Salmon-bronze with gold and pink suffusion.
Noël	Clear bronze with large flowers.
Oldland Bronze	Attractive orange-bronze.
Oldland Copper	A coppery pleasing shade.
Oldland Crimson	Good reddish-crimson.
Oldland Queen	Flowers are of a good shade and an attractive blush pink.
Oldland Rose	A rose-coloured Oldland.
Orange Ada Stevens	An orangy sport of Ada Stevens.
Pageant	Bright salmon-bronze overlaid gold.

BETTY WOOLMAN BROADACRE

SHIRLEY IVORY CRIMSON CROWN

Variety	*Description*
Peach Rose Harrison	A peach-coloured sport of Rose Harrison.
Pearl Loveliness	Delicate pearly-white shading to pink.
Peter John	Pearl-pink sport of Colham Pink.
Picture	Bright rose-pink with gold reverse.
Pink Favourite	Soft pink sport from Favourite.
Power	Peach pink to salmon shade.
Primrose Loveliness	A primrose sport of Loveliness.
Red Agnes Ford	A red sport of Agnes Ford.
Red Crensa	Rich chestnut-red variety.
Red Favourite	Light red sport of Favourite.
Red Finale	Reddish-bronze sport from Finale.
Red Fiona	Good bright red with reverse of gold.
Red Morris	Bright red sport of J. W. Morris.
Redwing	Bright crimson with gold reverse.
Rose Delight	Rich rose sport of Late Delight.
Rose Favourite	A rose sport of Favourite.
Rose Harrison	Delicate rose with green centre.
Rose Mollie Nicolson	Rose colour sport of Mollie Nicolson.
Rose Wallace	Attractive deep rose sport of Mary Wallace.
Royal Crensa	Rich cerise sport from Crensa.
Salmon Crensa	Salmon sport from Crensa.
Salmon Loveliness	A rich salmon sport of Loveliness.
Salmon Morris	Salmon sport of J. W. Morris.
Salmon Rose Harrison	A salmon sport of Rose Harrison.
Shell Beauty	A lovely shell pink.
Shirley Brilliant	Fine deep crimson.
Shirley Garnet	Garnet-crimson suffused carmine.
Shirley Ivory	Good ivory white.
Shirley Late Red	Very good late deep red.
Solomon	Excellent yellow.
Sovereign	Large stately golden-amber blooms.
Sussex Bronze	Good bronze of splendid growth.
Sussex Gold	Golden sport from Sussex Bronze.
Sussex Pink	Fine shade of light pink.
Sussex Red	Crimson-red with gold points.
Sussex Rose	Attractive soft rose.
Sussex White	Rich pink shade.
Sussex Yellow	Fine deep yellow.
Thanksgiving Pink	Excellent large pink from America.
Ulster	Large crimson-maroon with gold reverse.

I

Variety	Description
White Loveliness	Fine white sport with greenish centre.
White Rose	Pure-white sport from Rose Harrison.
White Wallace	Sport of May Wallace.
Winter Cheer	Deep rose-pink, suitable for spray.
Worthing Bronze	A grand bronze, flowers firm.
Worthing Gold	Rich old gold.
Worthing Red	One of the best reds, popular.
Worthing Success	Fine large medium pink with pointed petals.
Yellow Alston	Lemon-yellow sport from Edith Alston.
Yellow Favourite	A yellow sport of Favourite.
Yellow Finale	Very bright yellow sport from Finale.
Yellow Fiona	Golden yellow sport from Fiona.
Yellow Rose	Sport of White Rose of a most delicate pale yellow
Yellow Wallace	Clear canary-yellow sport from May Wallace.

Section VI. Incurving Decoratives

Variety	Description
Ace	Good golden-bronze.
Adonis	Salmon-pink with gold reverse.
American Beauty	Very fine white of good habit.
American Spartan	Another good large white.
Athene	Also a very pleasing white.
Avondale Beauty	Bright shell-pink, large flowers.
Balcombe Giant	Attractive golden yellow.
Balcombe Perfection	Broad-petalled flowers of amber-bronze.
Balcombe Shell	Rich shell-pink.
Bronze Adonis	Sport from Adonis of bright orange-bronze.
Cambria	Bronze variety similar to Coralie.
Constance Baker	Clear yellow, good for exhibition.
Coralie	Very beautiful shell-pink.
Cream Lady	Large attractive white.
Crimson Adonis	A plum-crimson sport of Adonis.
Dark Orchid Queen	Very deep pink sport of Orchid Queen.
Doris Moorcroft	Excellent light bronze.
Friendly Rival	The deepest yellow for Christmas.
Golden Ace	Golden bronze sport from Ace.
Golden Coralie	Rich golden sport of Coralie.
Golden Globe	Fine deep yellow.
Golden Pride	An attractive golden-yellow with large blooms.

Variety	Description
Hadley	Rose-red with lighter reverse.
Harry Shoesmith	New rich yellow variety.
Incurving Edith Alston	A pure white
Incurving White Favourite	An incurved sport of Favourite.
Indianapolis Bronze	Good light-bronze.
Indianapolis Pink	Very attractive pale rose-pink.
Indianapolis White	Excellent pure white for market.
Ivy Gay	Synonymous to Chieftain.
Jane Ignamells	Primrose sport from American Beauty.
Mary Dalling	Large pale pink flowers of good form.
Mont d'Or	A nice yellow, good style.
Mrs Roots	One of the purest whites.
Nobility	Pure yellow well-formed flowers.
October Rose	A grand October pink.
Oldland King	Compact medium bronze.
Pink Superb	Very clear pink.
Primrose Coralie	Sport of Coralie, of an excellent primrose.
Red Ace	Crimson sport of Ace.
Red Coralie	Another good sport of Coralie.
Red Hadley	Very distinct red sport of Hadley.
Rene	Sport from Coralie, buff-gold with centre of wine.
Ringleader	Pink with golden shading, unusual and attractive.
Rose Adonis	Very pleasing sport of Adonis.
Snow	Pure white well-formed blooms.
Southern Beauty	Deep chestnut sport of Ada Brooker.
Stiletto	Glistening yellow, lasts well.
Sunflash	Large bright amber blooms.
Sussex Pride	Rich pink shade – an improved Loveliness.
Sybil Chandler	Beautiful buff flowers with delicate shell-pink shading and light old gold reverse.
White Avondale	One of the best whites.
Worthing Jewel	Large rich ruby blooms.
Worthing Perfection	A beautiful rich golden bronze.
Yellow Ace	Excellent yellow sport from Ace.
Yellow American Beauty	Fine yellow sport from American Beauty.
Yellow Coralie	Quite a good yellow.

Section VII. Anemones
(a) Large-flowered

Variety	Description
Admiration	Deep rose shading to apricot cushion.
American Success	Deep lilac with cream lilac cushion
American Superb	Lilac pink. Yellow cushion
Antigo	Violet rose, bronze centre
Caleb Cox	Amber with golden-bronze cushion.
Cassino	Deep rose with paler cushion.
Descartes	Splendid crimson red.
Grace Land	White with a yellow cushion, excellent cut flower.
Norma	Pink with yellow cushion.
Ophelia	Rich deep gold sport from Caleb Cox. Most attractive.

(b) Medium-flowered

Aphrodite	A fine mauve pink slightly tipped gold. Very pretty.
Barbara Hilbury	Salmon-beige sport from Elspeth, suitable for spray.
Beautiful Lady	Delicate pink with cream cushion.
Beauty	White with lemon cushion.
Elspeth	Free flowering palish mauve-pink, suitable for spray.
Heloïse	Suitable for spray.
Mabel Weston	Pure white.
Marion Stacey	Rich old rose, white cushion.
Orbit	A charming sport from Heloïse, old-rose shaded salmon.
Thora	Deep rose with cream centre.

(c) Small-flowered (anemone) pompons

Golden Climax	Rich golden yellow.
Mrs Astie	Pale primrose.

Section VIII. Pompons
  (a) *Large-flowered*

Variety	Description
Dresden China	Shell-pink suffused lavender and gold.
Iridescent	A lovely pale-pink with a sheen.
Mdlle Elise Dordan	Attractive pink medium-sized blooms.

As well as Tansy, Terra-Cotta Bouquet and W. Sabey.

  (b) *Small-flowered*

Baby	Small rich yellow.
Dainty Maid	Pale pink.
Elmerinda	Lovely old rose with silver sheen.
Ethel	Fine reddish-bronze.
Francis Hutchinson	Rich claret shade.
Golden Climax	A yellow popular in the North.
Golden New York	A good little yellow.
Hilda Canning	Very fine bronze.
Mary Pickford	Attractive pale pink.
New York	Golden-bronze.
November Bronze	Bears beautiful light chestnut-bronze blooms.
Nugget	Very neat yellow blooms.
Padoka	Light-salmon.
Yellow Padoka	Small primrose-yellow.

Section IX. Singles
  (a) *Large-flowered*

Variety	Description
Audax	Broad stiff florets of an attractive pink.
Betty Woolman	Shining gold large florets.
Broadacre	Good pure white.
Bronze Dorothy	Bright bronze sport from Dorothy.
Bronze Fantasy	Fine bronze sport from Fantasy.
Bronze Molly	Apricot sport from Molly Godfrey.
Caroline	Extra large flowers of a most attractive clear pink.
Catriona	Rich old rose, with narrow white zone round golden eye.
Cleone	Large pleasing pale pink.
Cream	Charming soft cream exhibition variety.

Variety	Description
Crimson Collins	A delightful crimson – firm petals.
Crimson Crown	Fine bright crimson with yellow zone.
Deborah	Bright pink, excellent show variety.
Desert Chief	Golden amber.
Desert Moon	New yellow sport from Desert Song.
Desert Song	Attractive tawny-yellow with gold-tipped petals.
Dorothy	Large silky rose-pink blooms.
Dorothy Thomas	Pure white, the best white single to date.
Elena	Rich deep rose with white disc.
Empire	Good crimson with reverse of gold.
Fantasy	Fine rich amber.
Florence Statham	Straw-yellow; large flat exhibition flower.
G. H. Smart	Bright yellow with distinct green eye.
Golden Crown	Golden-bronze.
Golden Jinx	A pure gold.
Intensity	Extremely fine, deep yellow.
Invincible	Large crimson with yellow disc.
Janice	Fine deep rose-pink.
Jennifer	Golden yellow.
Jinx	One of the best whites.
Josephine Wells	Distinct rich glowing purple.
Lilian Jackson	Rose with clear-cut white disc.
Lisa	Very pretty rosy carmine.
Marius	Extremely fine white.
Mary Siddons	Improved crimson, new variety with medium yellow disc.
Molly Godfrey	Excellent deep pink.
Neil Dougal	Crimson with distinct yellow ring around the disc.
Pamela	First-class lemon-yellow.
Peter Robinson	Good exhibition yellow.
Prince Charming	Lovely old gold.
Quality	Deep rose with crimson sheen.
Red Banner	Distinctly reddish; good.
Red Molly	Deep chestnut-red sport of Bronze Molly.
Reginald Godfrey	Attractive russet-bronze.
Rivelin	Clear yellow.
Rob Roy	Crimson red with yellow ring.
Rose Molly	Sport of Molly Godfrey, deep rose.

Variety	Description
Royal Yellow	Excellent bright yellow.
Rubens	Deep rosy purple.
Satan	Very dark crimson.
Shirley Flame	Perfect scarlet-flame.
Shirley Gem	Large russet-bronze.
Shirley Sunrise	Beautiful yellow for Christmas.
Susan	Rose sport from Molly Godfrey.
Susette	Sport of Susan, attractive bronze shaded rose.
Yellow Cleone	Clear yellow sport of Cleone.
Yellow Supreme	Fine yellow of perfect shape.
Yellow Susan	A yellow sport of Susan.

(b) Medium-flowered

Artist	Very bright crimson.
Bronze Exmouth	Bronze sport of Exmouth pink, suitable for spray.
Bronze Phyllis Cooper	Lovely bronze sport of Phyllis Cooper.
Cheerio	Warm terra-cotta.
Chesswood Beauty	Bright crimson sport of Mason's Bronze.
Cleopatra	Fine terra-cotta bronze.
Dazzle	Rich velvety-crimson.
Exmouth Pink	A grand pink, suitable as spray.
Golden Mason's	Rich golden-yellow sport from Mason's Bronze.
Golden Seal	Very deep yellow, suitable as spray.
Ideal	Bright orange-red with yellow zone round centre.
Karen	Light orange-bronze.
Kate Park	Beautiful orange-yellow.
Mary Lee	Fine rich pink with firm petals.
Mason's Bronze	Very clear bronze.
Mason's Orange	Orange sport of Mason's Bronze.
Orange Glory	Orange on golden ground.
Orange Prince	Large orange-yellow.
Phyllis Cooper	Rich golden-yellow.
Pink Mason's	A pretty pink.
Pretty	Delightful pink with distinct white disc, suitable for spray.
Robin Hood	A red with bright green leaves.
Rowena	Excellent lemon-yellow.

Variety	Description
Ruth	Very good white.
Sabu	Rich rose, overlaid bronze.
Sonnie	Good deep-yellow.
Sphinx	Bright chestnut-scarlet.
Sunflower	Canary-yellow with very stiff petals.
Torch	New variety, yellow around disc, gradually deepening to orange suffused salmon at the tips.
Venita	Bright red with disc of yellow.

(c) Small-flowered

Godfrey's Gem	Warm golden apricot.
Market Gem	Bright crimson with yellow zone.

Section X. Spidery, Plumed and Feathery

Variety

Bertie Bindon
King of Plumes
Mrs Carter
Mrs Filkins
Sam Caswell
Sunkist

Section XI. Any other types

Variety	Description
Doc	A Lilliput of an attractive light rose.
Emu	Another Lilliput of deep pink with a purple suffusion.
Happy	A fine bright yellow of the Lilliput class.
Rayonnante	Attractive pink with frilled florets.
Redbreast	Very bushy red Lilliput.
Thrush	Yellow shaded with bronze, very compact Lilliput.
White Rayonnante	Beautiful white sport of Rayonnante.
Yellow Rayonnante	A beautiful delicate yellow sport of White Rayonnante.

OCTOBER-FLOWERING VARIETIES

Section XVI. Reflexed

(a) Large-flowered

Variety	Description
Amber Prince	Good light amber.
Balcombe Orange	Bright orange.
Balcombe Purity	Choice pure white
Blanche du Poitou	Very free-flowering creamy white.
Bounteous	Extremely attractive pink.
Bridgwater Gold	Intensely deep yellow or old gold.
Bronze Cranfordia	A bronzy sport of Cranfordia.
Bronze Smiles	Lovely bronze sport from Smiles.
Chairman	Flowers rather flat of a deep yellow.
Cranfordia	Good yellow which grows strongly and can be lifted with success.
Cranford Yellow	Very pure yellow – flowers profusely.
Graceful	Immense flowers of a beautiful mid-pink with gold centre.
Illustrious	Bright red of medium size.
Intense	New variety of a brilliant intense yellow.
John Wearing	Good orange-bronze.
Joyce	Attractive salmon-pink.
Mont Blanc	A nice white.
Mrs T. Riley	Very fine white.
New Countess	Rosy pink with golden reverse.
October Red	A reddish variety.
Pink Queen	A rather mauvy pink.
Primrose du Poitou	Attractive primrose sport from Blanche du Poitou.
Rose Queen	A good rose-coloured variety with a sheen.
Smiles	Salmon-pink with bronze shadings.
Snowdon	Very fine large white.
Stuart Ogg	New shade of soft salmon-pink.
Tempest	One of the best crimsons with old gold reverse.
Treasure	Broad thick golden-yellow florets.
William Greenyer	Large lilac-pink with stiff petals.
Yellow Hammer	Rich golden yellow.

(b) Medium-flowered

Variety	Description
Irene Shewell-Cooper	Glorious shade of deep amber. Excellent.
Joy Humphrey	New variety of a most attractive vermilion colour.
Primrose Beauty	A primrose shade, very attractive.
Yellow Gown	Produces excellent yellow blooms.

Section XVII. Incurving

(a) Large-flowered

Variety	Description
Dorothy Wilson	Rich canary yellow, of perfect form.
Forward	Silver peach-pink.
Ryecroft White	Large beautiful white, easy grower.
Topscore	Very early yellow.
Yellow Orb	Excellent rich yellow, a very good variety for market.

OUTDOOR VARIETIES

Section XX. Incurved

(a) Large-flowered

Variety	Description
Empire Primrose	Excellent sport from Empire White, good exhibition type.
Empire White	Very fine white.
George McLeod	First-class yellow of the Sutcliffe type but more refined.
Golden Circle	A gold circular flower.
Golden Sceptre	A 1950 golden-yellow, outstanding for exhibition.
Prefect	Another 1950 variety, pure white, a seedling from Empire White.
Shirley Cream	Very lovely cream.
Snow Queen	Produces white blooms of marvellous quality and size.
Symphony	Rosy-mauve outside petals with cream and lemon centre.
Yellow Shirley Cream	A yellow sport of Shirley Cream.

(b) Medium-flowered

Variety	Description
Alfreton Delight	Lovely shade of orange-bronze.
Alfreton Sunrise	Fine yellow.
Arctic Circle	Beautiful pure white.
Golden Crossley	Sport from the well-known E. Crossley.
Harvest Moon	Fine sport from Autumn Gold.
Mrs Irene Torrance	Very attractive yellow.
Primrose Circle	Sport of Arctic Circle, excellent light yellow.

(c) Small-flowered

Moonstone	White tinted cream, very good habit.

Section XXI. Reflexed

(a) Large-flowered

Variety	Description
Alaric	Large orange-bronze.
Alfreton Beauty	Brilliant orange-bronze.
Alfreton Ivory	Large ivory-white flowers of a very refined texture.
Amber Bright	Bright amber-bronze with rolled petals.
Arthur Ward	Very big amber-bronze, solid blooms.
Avalanche	One of the purest whites.
Balcombe Triumph	Bright red with reverse of light bronze.
Barbara	Pale rose-pink.
Betty Riley	Bright pink, centre of deeper colour.
Bronze Barbara	Light bronze sport from Barbara.
Bronze Marie	A bronze sport of Marie.
Carefree	Excellent chestnut-bronze for show.
Champion	Clear yellow blooms of large size.
Charter	Fine brown-bronze.
Claudius	Pale lilac with sheen of gold.
Conqueror	Rich deep crimson.
Corncob	Lovely shade of tangerine-orange.
Cream Duchess	Attractive cream shading to yellow in centre.
Dallas	Very large pink.
Dauntless	Rich bright orange-bronze with medium size flowers.
Daydream	Beautiful pale salmon colour.

Variety	*Description*
Débutante	Immense pure white.
Delia	Medium rose-pink.
Diane	Mauve-pink, excellent show variety.
Dorothy Speat	Glorious shade of pink with golden salmon centre.
Dorothy Wearing	1950 variety of rose-pink with gold centre.
Elsenham White	Synonymous to Débutante.
Fair Maid	Beautiful blush of grand texture.
Felicity	Pure white, very large blooms.
Flavius	Large buff-yellow.
Freda Pearce	Soft rose-pink with yellow and gold suffusions.
Gladys Case	Deep lilac-pink with silver reverse.
Golden Harvest	Fine large yellow.
Hope Valley	Extremely large lilac-pink.
Imperial Yellow	Immense yellow flowers.
Joan Fellowes	Seedling from Barbara of a rosy-cerise.
June Manser	Massive pale pink blooms.
Lady Mayoress	Synonymous to Dallas.
Marie	Syonymous to Lady Mayoress and Dallas.
Marion	White shading to a centre of canary-yellow.
Mayford Orange	Bright amber-bronze, one of the best of its colour.
Mayford Pink	Extremely large bright rose with bright gold centre.
Mayford Red	Deep rich red.
Mayland Yellow	Fine large yellow.
Monsal Dale	Cream with a flush of pink, free and strong.
Monsal Head	Bright terra-cotta bronze with gold reverse.
New Sanctuary	White tinged with cream.
Nomad	Golden-amber.
Orange Torch	Golden orange with gold reverse.
Pink Pearl	Seedling from Sweetheart of a soft pearl-salmon shade.
Phœbus	Rich yellow with rolled petals.
Polar Beauty	Extra large white of great substance.
Primrose Barbara	Sport from Barbara of a beautiful primrose.
Purple King	Immense purple variety.
Red Zenith	Distinct sport from Zenith.
Rosevern	1950 variety of deep clover.
Royal Pink	Clear pink, well-formed blooms.

Variety	Description
September Red	Fine sport from August Red.
Serenus	Extra large white flowers.
Sunburst	Excellent variety for exhibition, golden base marked with orange and red.
Vanity	Strawberry with cream shading.
Viking	Orange-bronze with gold reverse.
Winsome	Lovely bright rosy-purple.
Yellow Barbara	Rich yellow sport of Barbara.
Zenith	Rich purple-maroon.

(b) Medium-flowered

Variety	Description
Adama	Grand yellow of excellent habit.
Alabaster	Very early white.
Alfreton Yellow	Fine golden-yellow sport from Alfreton Beauty.
Alfreton Yeoman	Maroon with silver reverse.
Alpine	Pure white of medium size.
Amber Crown	Light golden-amber.
Amber Utopia	An amber-coloured sport of Utopia.
Amber Vale	Golden amber, broad-pointed petals.
Ansom	Soft shell-pink large blooms.
Apricot Sweetheart	A very true apricot, suitable for spray.
Arnhem	Large terra-cotta.
August Pink	Fine clear pink.
August Red	Immense blooms.
Autumn Gold	Good deep yellow.
Balcombe Brilliance	Brilliant red flowers.
Balcombe Supreme	Bright red with gold reverse.
Bravado	A fine crimson-scarlet with golden-bronze reverse.
Bronze Amber Vale	Bright bronze sport of Amber Vale.
Bronze Sweetheart	Chestnut-bronze with gold centre and reverse, suitable as spray. Sport of Sweetheart.
Bulwark	Large chestnut-bronze blooms.
Capable	Beautiful reddish-crimson.
Carol	Deep rose-pink with gold reverse.
Challenger	Bronze-red.
Chastity	Pure glistening white.
Chatsworth	1950 variety of copper-bronze.
Chestnut Gem	Attractive light chestnut shade.

Variety	Description
Christine Sweetheart	Delightful strawberry sport from Sweetheart.
Clerepink	Glorious shade of pink.
Copper Utopia	A coppery sport of Utopia.
Corona	Buff shaded orange.
Cotswold Bronze	Orange-bronze of medium size.
Cotswold Gem	Excellent white for spray.
Cotswold Pink	Rich clear pink.
Cotswold White	Grand white with glossy petals.
Delicacy	1950 variety of an attractive shade of pink.
Dollars	Flowers of a beautiful old-gold shade.
Edale	Salmon-pink.
Edensor	Creamy white, ideal for market.
Effective	Golden amber with gold reverse.
Egerton Sweetheart	Salmon-bronze sport from Sweetheart, suitable as spray.
Elsie Carter	Fine shining purple.
Falaise	Scarlet crimson with gold reverse.
Flaming Torch	Lovely bright crimson-scarlet.
Fortune	Grand white of exceptional quality.
Gladiator	Large chestnut-crimson.
Gold of Ophir	A lovely gold.
Hurricane	Brilliant crimson
Jean Pickering	Fine large bronze.
Ladybower	Rose-pink with flowers of good texture.
Ladylike	Light-salmon variety, 1950 introduction.
Lovelace	Attractive shell-pink.
Mary Mona	Salmon-cerise.
Mauve Princess	Deep mauve flowers.
Mayford Triumph	Bright scarlet-bronze variety.
Merrydew	1950 scarlet-bronze with gold reverse.
Miller's Dale	One of the purest whites.
Orange Lovelace	A good orange – disbuds.
Orange Sweetheart	Beautiful orange, suitable as spray.
Peach Sweetheart	Attractive shade of peach.
Pearl	Lovely pale-pink.
Pearl Sweetheart	One of the Sweetheart family, pearl deepening to salmon-pink at centre.
Pirate	Bright crimson with gold centre.
Prelude	Flaming bronze with gold reverse.
Prima Donna	1950 variety with wide petals and a good white.

Variety	*Description*
Purity	Pure white of outstanding merit.
Radar	Excellent golden-bronze.
Red Flare	Rich red with gold reverse, 1950 introduction.
Red Royal	A good red.
Red Sweetheart	Sport from Sweetheart, soft red with gold reverse, suitable as spray.
Revenge	An immense, very full flower of crimson, the petals are tipped with gold.
Ronald	Attractive new rich plum-crimson.
Rose Princess	Deep rose-pink.
Royal Bronze	Rich orange-scarlet.
Royal Flame	1950 introduction, red with golden reverse.
Royal Prince	Bright orange-bronze seedling from Royal Bronze.
Ruby	Colour as name, beautifully shaped plant.
Salmon Lovelace	Bright salmon sport of Lovelace.
Salmon Sweetheart	Very good sport, even stronger than Sweetheart.
Sanctity	Pure white, can be used as spray.
September Bronze	A good bronze, flowers as a rule mid-September.
September Rose	Bright rose-pink.
Serenade	Charming soft shade of pink.
Spartan	Very brilliant with a centre of clear gold.
Stella	Excellent clear pink, free flowering.
Sunbeam	Attractive bright yellow.
Sweetheart	Rose-pink, tinged gold with a flush of cream, suitable as spray.
Tibshelf Glory	Orange-bronze.
Tibshelf Orange	Rich bright orange.
Typhoon	Good rich crimson.
Utopia	Fine yellow-bronze.
Valentine	Large pure white.
Vanguard	Rich crimson-bronze with gold reverse.
White Ensign	An outstanding white.
Yellow Corona	Clear yellow sport from Corona.
Yellow Utopia	From the well-known variety Utopia.
Youth	Delightful clear pink, very suitable variety for market.

(c) Small-flowered

Variety	Description
Bronze Freda	Bright bronze sport of Freda, suitable as spray.
Colleen	Bronze-yellow.
Crimson Firedrake	A lovely red, suitable as spray.
Dorothy Vernon	Pink rolled petals, attractive yellow centre, suitable as spray.
Flaming Beauty	Copper crimson with reverse of gold.
Freda	Fine pink, suitable as spray.
Golden Gem	Bright yellow, suitable as spray.
Lidice	Very good bronze.
Luminous	Scarlet terra-cotta.
Madeleine	Beautiful clear shell-pink, long fluted and pointed petals.
Phœnix	Suitable as spray.
Pluie d'Argent	Almost like silver, a good spray variety.
Red Crusader	Quite a good red, excellent for spray.
Red Osprey	A fine spray variety of a bright red.
Salmon Freda	Very pretty sport of Freda, pale salmon, suitable as spray.
Snowfall	Lovely white spray variety.
Sparkler	Bright crimson variety for spray.
Terra-Cotta Freda	A terra-cotta sport of Freda, good for spray.
Wendy	Good orange amber, suitable for spray.
Yellow Argent	A good yellow, first class for spray.
Yellow Wendy	Deep yellow sport from Wendy, used for spray.

Section XXII. Incurving

(a) Large-flowered

Variety	Description
Ajax	Golden-bronze.
Bronze Early Buttercup	Rich deep bronze with reverse of golden-buff.
Bronze McLeod	Good bronze sport of George McLeod.
Bronze Una	Pleasing bronze sport of Una.
Crimson Buttercup	Sport of Bronze Early Buttercup, crimson with bronze reverse.
E. Crossley	Intense mahogany with reverse of gold.

PEACH UNA

ROYAL PRINCE

SOLIDITY

MILTON GRAY

Facing +

Variety	Description
Golden Surprise	A grand yellow of good constitution.
H. Sutcliffe	Sport from Bronze Early Buttercup – golden-yellow.
High Command	Deep mahogany-red with gold reverse.
Incurved Zenith	Distinct sport from Zenith, good for exhibition.
Lady Electra	An excellent white.
Peach Una	Very attractive sport from Una.
Pink Una	A pink sport of Una.
Red McLeod	Fine sport from George McLeod.
Salmon Una	Another pleasing sport from Una.
Silver Queen	A lovely silvery pink.
Trevor Adams	Massive clear-chrome yellow.
Una	Pink with silver reverse.

Section XXIII. Singles

(a) Large-flowered

Variety	Description
Autumn Glow	As its name suggests – a glowing bronze.
Edith	Attractive rosy pink.
Jean	Fine new variety of orange terra-cotta.
Kitty	Very large rose with a white yoke.
Major Robertson	Crimson-scarlet, suitable for exhibition.
Marvo	Chestnut with yellow ring.
Red Riding Hood	A good red.
Richard Holding	Intense chestnut-scarlet with bright yellow centre.
Rodney	Good shade of bronze.
Snowstorm	Pure white flowers with a green centre.
Supreme	Massive yellow, good for exhibition.

(b) Medium-flowered

Caradoc	Fine yellow.
Clyro	Another yellow with long stem and grand for spray.
Columbine	Rose-strawberry variety.
Doreen Woolman	Intense golden-orange.
Firebrand	Long elegant sprays of terra-cotta red flowers.
Fire King	Bright crimson-red.
Golden Gleam	A glorious yellow.

K

Variety	Description
Keith	Produces a mass of yellow blooms.
Nectar	Beautiful almond-blossom pink.
Orient	Very pleasing rich gold shading to amber.
Salmonea	A salmon-coloured kind.
September Gem	Clear yellow in huge clusters.
Shirley Charming	Attractive shade of pink.
Shirley Crimson	Rich crimson with golden-yellow disc.
Shirley Terra Cotta	A terra-cotta Shirley, as its name suggests.
Vicar of Shirley	

Section XXIV. Pompons

(a) Tall

Variety	Description
Babs	Dainty light-pink.
Cream Bouquet	Small neat blooms on long stems.
Dandy	Shell-pink pointed florets with green centre.
Fawn Bouquet	Fine fawn with gold centre.
Golden Bouquet	Very rich fine yellow variety.
Janté Wells	Bright golden-yellow.
Judy	Pretty lilac.
Mosquito	Very compact flowers of a beautiful yellow.
Pink Bouquet	Attractive clear pink.
Punch	Very bright orange-bronze.
Purple Bouquet	A purply shade.
Salmon Bouquet	Attractive rosy-salmon.
Shell Bouquet	A pleasing shell-pink.
Snow Elf	An excellent pure white.
White Bouquet	Small flattish blooms of pure white.
Yellow Bouquet	Small flattish blooms yellow in colour.

(b) Dwarf

Anastasia	Good purple.
Bopeep	Pale blush ground shading to crimson at centre.
Bronze Anastasia	Bronze sport of Anastasia.
Gentillesse	Cream, pink blush.
Piercy's Seedling	Bronzy yellow.
Scarlet Gem	A grand little scarlet variety.
Toreador	A fine red.
White St Crouts	An excellent white.

CHAPTER XV

The Less Usual Types:
Anemone-Centred, Cascades, Charms, Koreans, Lilliputs and Others

THERE are a number of less usual types of chrysanthemums that may be grown with great success, even by a beginner. Generally speaking, the kinds mentioned in this chapter have their devotees because most of them are quite easy to grow and are extremely effective either in the garden or, in some cases, as pot plants. Some, like the Charms and Cascades, can easily be raised by seed sowing; others, like the Koreans, are usually propagated by cuttings.

The Cascades are particularly pretty because, as their name suggests, they cascade down to the ground if they are grown in pots high enough up. I never think of Cascades or Charms without being grateful to my friend Mr A. P. Balfour, of Sutton's, who has done so much to popularise these two kinds.

ANEMONE-CENTRED

The Anemone-Centred chrysanthemums are either tremendously admired or are intensely disliked; it all depends on the gardener's taste. They came originally from America, and latterly a number of Anemone-Centred singles have been introduced from the U.S.A. In most cases the disc florets are of quite a different colour from the ray florets, with the result that interesting contrasts are produced. For instance, you get a golden bronze cushion with a brick-red surround, or a creamy cushion with a deep lilac surround, and so on.

Most gardeners cultivate the Anemone-Centred varieties in exactly the same way as the singles described in Chapter XII, but those who are going in for showing will like to know that it is usual to make two stoppings, the first about March 15th, and the second about June 15th. Only two shoots are allowed after the first stopping, and another two shoots after the second stopping, making four in all.

Most varieties grow about 4½ feet tall, but it is possible to get from a good nurseryman some which are dwarfer and can therefore be grown, if desired, in pots. In the case of pot culture, follow the instructions given in Chapter X.

In the South, at any rate, it is possible to grow the plants in the border and to have them flowering in normal years in November. In very wet seasons they may require some protection, such as a length of butter muslin stretched over the plants and held in position by temporary posts driven into the ground.

Anemone-Centred varieties will live through a frost as a rule, and if grown in the open they could be dug up in October and planted in a greenhouse, or if preferred, a dutch-light house could be erected over them where they grow. It much depends, of course, on the numbers and whether one is growing for market or just for household use.

Varieties

Variety	Description
Admiration	Rose shaded apricot cushion, with deep rose petals around, large.
American Gain	Excellent brick-red with a cushion of golden-bronze.
American Schlager	Very pretty variety of a glorious shade of amber.
American Selecta	Purple shaded to red with a bronze cushion.

Variety	Description
American Success	Produces large deep lilac flowers with cream lilac cushion.
American Superb	Lilac-pink with soft yellow cushion.
Beautiful Lady	Dwarf, excellent for pots, cream cushion, pale pink petals.
Caleb Cox	Large amber with cushion of golden-bronze.
Cassino	Strong grower, pale pink cushion, deep rose petals.
Grace Land	White with yellow cushion.
Marion Stacey	1950 introduction of rich old rose with white cushion.

CASCADES

These delightful small-flowered single chrysanthemums are rapidly regaining their pre-war popularity. Because of the ease with which they can be trained in the tumbling or cascade form, they have been named the 'Cascade Chrysanthemum', but when grown naturally the plant forms a bush like any other chrysanthemum.

The plants, which come into flower at the end of October and continue into December, are very decorative and useful as cut flowers.

The colours range from white to pale pink, rose-pink, shades of yellow, bronze, red and crimson, and many of the flowers are delicately scented.

Culture

Plants are easily raised from seed, which should be sown in gentle heat in early February, the resulting seedlings when large enough being pricked out into boxes and potted on as required, or pricked out direct into 3-inch pots, later into 5-inch pots, and finally into 9- or 10-inch pots by early May. As soon as the weather is genial the plants should be put outside in an open, sunny yard, sheltered if possible from high wind.

Stopped once in the early stages to ensure branching, large freely branching plants are produced, 3 to 5 feet in height and as much across, and covered with bloom. The following soil composts are used at the various stages of growth.

Seed sowing

The John Innes Seed Compost should be used.

For the final potting compost use the John Innes Potting Compost No. 2.

It is very important to give adequate watering and feeding once the final pots are full of roots. These chrysanthemums are gross feeders and must be regularly top-dressed with a suitable fertiliser. It is also a good thing to change the feeding, which can be given with other materials such as Liquinure. Precautions must be taken against the usual chrysanthemum pests and diseases, such as leaf miner, mildew, aphis, capsid, etc.; in other words, the same kind of treatment as for the growing of specimen plants of Japanese chrysanthemums.

Training methods

The following is a brief description of some of the ways in which this very useful plant can be trained:

For specially trained plants, whether in the 'Cascade' or any other form, definite separate colours are usually required, and for this purpose plants from cuttings must be used, which are usually taken in early January. Seed will give equally good results if no particular colour is required.

In all cases stopping should cease around September 10th, and during the third or fourth week of the month the plants should be brought in under cover in a greenhouse with a little heat if possible.

Cascades. This special training consists in reducing the

plant to one or two leading shoots at an early stage. Pots
are then placed upon a shelf or in a trough in front of a
hedge or wall, facing south, from $4\frac{1}{2}$ to 6 feet above the
ground. A bamboo stake should be secured to the root at
an angle just off the perpendicular, down which the leading
shoot, or shoots, may then be trained (Fig. 1). All laterals
are stopped at two or three leaves, and stopped again as
required to make bushy lateral growth – the leader being
allowed to grow on – and tied to the bamboo stake as
growth progresses. Attention should be given to this pro-
cedure every few days during the growing season. At the
end of September the stakes should be removed and the pots
placed on a shelf or pedestal in the cool greenhouse, when
the plants will be from 4 to 6 feet long. When in position
in the house it is advisable to fix the ends of the longest
shoots to some support to prevent the plants being damaged.

Standards. When making the final potting it is important
that a good strong stake should be firmly planted right to
the bottom of the pot, and rising to a height of 3 feet
above the rim (Fig. 2). It is on this stake that the leader is
trained, and in due course it will have to support the head
of the plant.

From the beginning the leader should be given freedom
of growth, pinching out all side shoots until a height of
about 2 to 3 feet is reached, when the leader is stopped. Two
or three side shoots are then allowed to develop, and it is a
question of stopping and re-stopping every two or three
leaves to build up a 'mop'-like head.

The building-up process continues until the first or
second week in September.

During the period when the plants are being trained
outside on the ashes it is well to have the supporting stakes
tied to a cross wire to prevent the wind blowing the plants
over, especially when the head is developing.

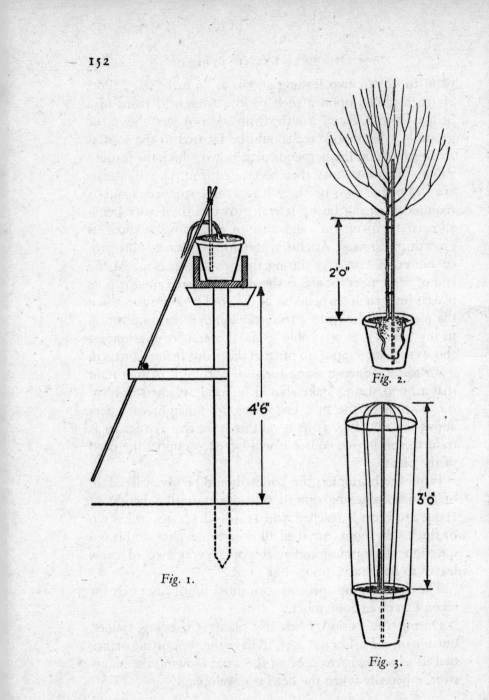

Fig. 1.

Fig. 2.

Fig. 3.

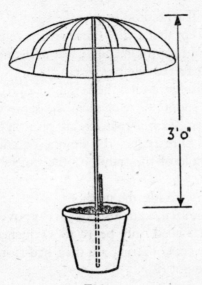

Fig. 4.

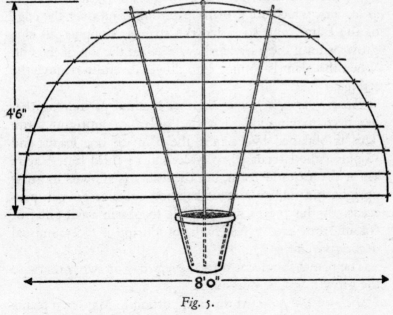

Fig. 5.

Umbrellas. The method here is the same as for the 'standard' form, except that a wire frame, shaped like the cover of an umbrella and approximately 3 feet in diameter, is secured to the stage 3 feet above pot level (Fig. 4).

When the leader reaches the height of $2\frac{1}{2}$ feet, it is stopped and the side shoots developed in the same way as for the 'standard' form, except that in this case they are kept tied down to the wire frame, the object, of course, being to cover the whole of the frame by the time stopping ceases in September.

Weeping forms. As in the method for the 'umbrella' form, a wire frame is secured to a stake 3 feet above pot level, but the wire frame need only be 12 to 15 inches in diameter. Six to eight pieces of string are then tied from the frame to the top of the pot (Fig. 3).

Like the 'umbrella' form, the leader is stopped at about $2\frac{1}{2}$ feet, and the aim then is at getting six to eight side shoots as leaders, which are grown up through and over the edge of the frame, and so down the strings, stopping all side growths until these leaders have reached the top of the pot. When the plant is coming into flower carefully remove the strings.

Pillar or upright forms. Another method of training that has been much admired is the 'pillar' or 'upright' form. This is obtained by keeping the plant to one leader and stopping the laterals at every second or third leaf, exactly as for the 'cascade' form, but the leader is allowed to grow upright and tied to a stout bamboo stake as growth proceeds. By this means it is possible to obtain a tall pillar of colour from 4 to 7 feet high, producing a most unusual decorative effect.

The plants should be turned every day or two, otherwise the growth will be one-sided.

'Fan-trained' form. At the final potting in May, two plants

of the same colour (or two different colours if desired) should be potted on side by side in the one pot.

When potting, three stout bamboo stakes should also be fixed in the pot, one dead centre rising to a height of $4\frac{1}{2}$ feet, and the other two down the sides of the pot, thus giving as wide an angle at the top as possible.

These three stout bamboos are used as the foundation for the thinner horizontal canes, which should be tied on about 6 inches apart, starting about 3 inches above the rim of the pot (Fig. 5).

The bottom cane should be at least 8 feet across, and each succeeding cane should be slightly shorter as they rise, so as to make as near as possible a half-circle, or fan.

The plants should be first stopped at about 6 inches, and from then on it is a question of stopping to get as many leaders and side shoots as are necessary to build up the fan and to fill in all spaces as the plant grows.

Messrs Sutton and Sons Ltd., of Reading, were pioneers in the introduction, selection and breeding of Cascade and Charm Chrysanthemums. They have carried out an immense amount of experimental work with these plants, mainly at their Slough Experimental Station; selections of them running into many thousands and occupying considerable glasshouse space. It is largely due to these efforts and consequent improvement in habit of plant and colour of flower that both the Cascade and Charm type Chrysanthemums have become so popular with the amateur and professional gardeners in this country.

CHARMS

Seed should be sown in gentle heat in February, and as soon as large enough the plants should be pricked out into 60-size pots and stopped by pinching out the growing point at the third or fourth leaf. No further stopping or training is necessary and, as the plants develop, no staking or support of any kind is required. A fortnight later they should be potted into 48-size pots, and about the end of May or early in June transferred into the final pots – 8-inch, 9-inch, or 10-inch, according to the size of plants required.

After the final potting, the pots should be placed outside, preferably on ashes. An open situation should be chosen, but exposure to high winds should be avoided. Towards the end of September or early in October, when the plants begin to show flower buds, they should be given the protection of a cool greenhouse. A completely cold house will be found quite sufficient to flower these plants well, but should the weather become very bad a slight amount of heat in the pipes is an advantage in maintaining a buoyant atmosphere and thus avoiding mildew. Free ventilation must be given at all times. The plants will come into flower towards the end of October and continue nearly to Christmas.

For sowing the seeds we advise a normal light compost of 2 parts loam, 1 part leaf-mould and 1 part sand, with about 1 ounce of lime to each bushel of soil. The same soil may be used for potting into the 60-size pots, but for the 48-size pots an extra part of loam should be added. For the final potting the compost should contain 7 parts loam, 2 parts leaf-mould, 1 part well-rotted farmyard manure and 1 part coarse sand.

As this chrysanthemum is a gross feeder, top-dressing is necessary to get the finest results. When the pots have become filled with roots, which is usually about four weeks after the final potting, a weekly feed is an advantage. Use Liquinure Flower Special or a good fish fertiliser for the purpose. Feeding must stop about the middle of September. Careful watch should be kept for the usual chrysanthemum pests and spraying with nicotine carried out as necessary.

For small plants

Smaller but equally attractive plants can be obtained by sowing seed up to the middle of April in a cold frame or greenhouse. When large enough, the seedlings should be pricked off into 60-size pots, with a final potting into the 5- or 6-inch size. It will be found advantageous to plunge the pots in ashes up to the rim to help conserve moisture and thus avoid continuous watering. This method will produce well-furnished plants to flower at about the same time as larger specimens.

KOREANS

It was in 1936 that I first saw the Korean, and then this new race caused quite an excitement. It seems that they originally came to this country from America as the result of Mr Harland P. Kelsey collecting them from the northern part of Korea in 1921. Mr Kelsey carried out in the U.S.A. a good deal of crossing with the best free-flowering varieties of the early chrysanthemums, and the result has been the Korean hybrid, which will put up with almost any frost and which flowers magnificently in the autumn. Unlike other kinds of chrysanthemum, it is possible to leave the roots in the open ground all the winter.

Various nurserymen such as Messrs Wells, and Messrs Simpson, have had much to do with the introduction of good varieties, and there are some first-class pastel shades available at the moment.

Cuttings and planting out

It is usual to take cuttings of Koreans as late as in March and to strike these in sandy soil in frames or under cloches so that the plants are ready to put out in the open early in May. Those who have no frames or cloches may adopt just the ordinary method of digging up the clumps and dividing them in the spring.

The little plants usually produce their first buds about 12 inches from ground-level, and then lateral growths develop. It is seldom one has to do any stopping at all. The stems are very wiry and strong, and some varieties grow to a height of 18 inches and others to a height of 2½ feet. The great advantage of Koreans is perhaps that they can be allowed to grow quite naturally without any securing of buds or disbudding at all.

General remarks

Manure and feed the land as advised for ordinary chrysanthemums because Koreans are rather greedy. Be prepared to stake the taller varieties with a bamboo, but the dwarfer kinds will usually stand up quite stiffly without any support at all. The taller varieties will need planting about 2 feet apart and dwarfer kinds may go in as close as 18 inches square, and if planted in this way they produce a perfect mass of bloom which completely hides the soil.

For those who like plants for cutting Koreans are ideal. You can either cut the stem low down and so bring into the house a magnificent 'spray' display which looks most natural in a vase, or if preferred the individual branches may be cut, the stems being quite long enough for modern vases.

Varieties

Variety	Description
Aphrodite	A very pleasing pink.
Apollo	An attractive bronze-red single.
Astrid	Pale pink single, very bushy.
Diana	Warm pink.
Daphne	Produces excellent salmon-pink blooms.
Ember	Semi-double bronze.

Variety	*Description*
Janté Wells	Golden yellow double, dwarf, excellent for garden or pots.
King Midas	A bronze tipped with yellow.
Louis Schilling	Crimson single, tall, strong grower.
Mars	A deep amaranth overlaid with the richest of red-wine tints.
Mercury	Bronze-red.
Romany	Fine reddish-bronze, double.
Saturn	Good orange-bronze.
The Moor	A double amaranth.
Venus	Deep salmon-pink.

LILLIPUTS

This section is by no means completely hardy. It is necessary to dig the stools up early in the winter and plant them in frames or in a cold greenhouse. Cuttings can then be taken in January and February in the normal way. There are perhaps few types of chrysanthemums which are more easily attacked by eelworm than Lilliputs, and therefore after lifting all stools should be given the warm-water treatment as advised on page 29.

The plants as a whole are very dwarf, and so they are often used in a similar way to the baby Michaelmas daisies – in fact, they mix quite well with these plants in drifts and are often used for an autumn display as 'edgers'. Some gardeners have planted them in rock gardens, others have used them rather like bedding plants for the autumn. They will grow satisfactorily in almost any soil.

Once the cuttings have struck, grow the plants on with a little protection, say, in a frame until mid-May, and then plant them out where they are to grow, and without any stopping, staking or special treatment, they will produce a mass of flowers for quite a long period. The blooms are, as a rule, anything from 1 inch to $1\frac{1}{2}$ inches across. Plants may, however, produce five hundred flowers each!

Varieties

Variety	*Description*
Bashful	Reddy-bronze, free flowering, September/October.
Doc	Produces a perfect mound of rose-pink flowers, August/September.
Doris	Lilac-blush, compact, September.
Emu	Not unlike Doc, with a purple suffusion to the pink flowers, September.
Happy	A clear yellow profusion of blooms, August.
Honeybird	Glowing orange-amber which lasts well, September/October.
Horus	Light pink, double, September.
Pheasant	The blooms are of a pale strawberry with a conspicuous anemone centre, September.
Pimpernel	A glowing chestnut form of this delightful section, September.
Redbreast	Beautiful red, free flowering, September.
Thetis	Bright orange, anemone centre, October.
Thrush	Compact bronzy yellow, October.
Tom Tit	Maize yellow, October/November.

PERPETUALS

I remember first seeing these chrysanthemums at the Chelsea Show before the war. They grow from 8 to 12 inches high and they produce a mass of flowers 3 or 3½ inches across. The great advantage of this variety is that it goes on flowering almost all through the year.

The plan is to root the cuttings in January and about five weeks later to pot them up into 3-inch pots containing the J.I.P. Compost No. 1. These plants are usually in flower about the middle of March. Directly the pots are full of roots potting on is done into 5-inch pots, the compost this time being the J.I.P. Compost No. 2. They can go on growing in these pots if necessary, or better still, they can be planted out in the open ground about the middle of May.

After the first set of flowers has been cut fresh shoots

develop from the base of the plant which also flower satisfactorily and the plants go on doing this month after month. As a result, the market gardener finds them useful for wreath work or to sell as pot plants later in the year. The private gardener and amateur like them because they are useful for house decoration at almost any time.

As regards feeding, treat them as if they were early-flowering chrysanthemums (see Chapter VIII).

Varieties

Variety	Description
*Perpetual White	A perfect white, apt to be a little shaggy.
*Perpetual Yellow	A lovely yellow sport which has a similar habit of growth.

POMPONES, POMPOMS, OR POMPONS

These chrysanthemums are said to have been quite popular in the Victorian era. Then when the bigger types came in they were neglected, and now they are coming into popularity once more. They are called 'Pompoms' in some parts of the country, 'Pompons' in other districts, and even 'Pompones'. All the plants are dwarf in habit of growth, and all the flowers are double and tend to be round in shape.

As a group, the plants are all very hardy and they grow happily in the open. Some gardeners have potted up a few specimens and brought them into the house for decoration, and there is no reason why this should not be done, especially with the October-flowering kinds.

There are no particular instructions as regards cultivation. The plants will grow in any good soil. They can be treated in exactly the same manner as the Koreans (see page 155). There is no stopping or disbudding to do. As to propaga-

* Synonymous with Clive d'Argent and Yellow d'Argent.

tion by cuttings, this can be done in the usual way (see Chapter V, page 34).

Varieties

See Classification List of Varieties on page 133.

RUBELLUM CHRYSANTHEMUMS
(*Chrysanthemum Rubellum*)

It is said that this section can be considered halfway between the Lilliputs and the Koreans. Certainly the plants are all free flowering, and they grow in a bushy manner 2 or 3 feet in height. They are absolutely hardy and they generally come through an 'arctic' winter without any losses at all. All the Rubellums are free flowering, and they are just as useful for the flower border or to use as bedding plants. Some gardeners grow them in pots for decoration in the house; others concentrate on them as cut flowers, and they last particularly well in water.

There is no difficulty at all in propagating Rubellums, either from cuttings taken in March in sandy soil in a frame or by means of division of established plants. If preferred, one can leave the plants where they are growing over the winter and then just thin out the growths that appear in the spring. Some have left them in a border for three years before splitting them up under such conditions.

They appreciate being grown on soil which has been enriched with plenty of organic matter, and prior to planting out, a good fish manure with a 5 per cent potash content should be lightly forked in at 3 to 4 ounces to the square yard. In cases where the plants are to remain in a border for three years, it is as well each March to apply a dressing of fish manure at a similar rate.

There is no stopping or disbudding to carry out; the

plants may be allowed to grow naturally, when they will produce an absolute mass of single flowers.

Varieties

Variety	Description
Anna Hay	A shell-pink, $2\frac{1}{2}$ feet.
Deborah Hollingworth	A coppery bronze, $2\frac{1}{2}$ feet.
Dorothy Thompson	A dark rose enhanced by a snow-white ring surrounding the golden yellow centre, $2\frac{1}{2}$ feet.
Duchess of Edinburgh	A glowing red, flowers last perfectly for weeks, 3 feet.
Ffrida	A luminous pink, strong upright stems, late September, 3 feet.
Jarvis Bay	Rosy red, compact, bushy, 3 feet.
Mary Stoker	Soft canary yellow, vigorous, $2\frac{1}{2}$ feet.
Moira Goddard	Soft shell pink, lasts well in water, $2\frac{1}{2}$ feet.
Nancy Perry	A lovely old rose, free flowering, 2 feet.
Paul Boissier	Orange bronze, free flowering, 3 feet.
Princess Margaret	Orchid pink, very branchy, mid-September/October, 3 feet.
Royal Enfield	Rich oriental red, shading to coral, coppery tones on petal reverse, $2\frac{1}{2}$ feet.
Spitfire	Carmine red, shades to garnet-crimson as the flower matures, $2\frac{1}{2}$ feet.

CHAPTER XVI

Chrysanthemum Diseases and Pests

I HAVE tried to make it very clear in a previous book of mine, *The ABC of Garden Pests and Diseases*, that 'troubles' have appeared to increase rather than decrease in the last twenty years or so because we are very international in the exchange of plants and because the advent of the aeroplane has brought countries far closer together. Despite all restrictions, diseases and pests do spread. They may be brought over on the fuselage of air liners, or on the decks of tramp steamers, or even on the legs of migratory birds.

Furthermore, in the days of yore the larger estates had plenty of gardeners whose job it was to grow the best crops and to keep the diseases and pests down. The working man had very little garden. Nowadays, every house worth calling a house has a good garden, but unfortunately it is not every owner who bothers to control diseases and pests. In many cases, therefore, a garden may become a breeding ground for all kinds of troubles. As against all this, the modern gardener has great advantages over those who had to do similar work fifty years ago. There are new insecticides and fungicides, and biologists have studied the life histories of most 'troubles', and so we now know when to spray and what to spray with.

We must all of us start though with the care of the soil. Plants need feeding properly in exactly the same way as human beings. If humans are ill-nourished they are much more subject to diseases than when they are properly fed. See, therefore, that the instructions given in the earlier chapters on feeding the plants are carefully carried out, and if you do you will never have the same need to use insecticides and fungicides as when the plants are starved.

Half the battle of trying to cure a disease or kill a pest is being able to diagnose the trouble correctly. Do not, for instance, try to kill with poison an insect that obtains its food by sucking the sap right in the middle of the leaf or stem. You can only poison insects that actually eat leaves or stems, like caterpillars. Buy a good magnifying glass so that you can examine the plants carefully and make up your mind whether the trouble is due to a pest or a fungus disease. Then learn to apply the right remedy in the correct manner at the right time. There is usually one vulnerable stage in the life history of any 'enemy', and if the cure can be applied then, all will be well. To dust or spray before or after the critical period may be quite useless.

FUNGUS DISEASES

It can be said (though the scientist will say that it is not absolutely true) that a fungus disease can be likened to a plant growing on another plant. It produces little branches which, of course, are the part of the disease the gardener sees. These produce little sacks of seed, or spores as they are called, which in their turn blow about and land on leaves or stems, where they germinate and send their little roots (or 'mycelia', as they should be called) into the plant tissue. The fungus is then established and will produce more branches, more sacks of spores, and so the disease will spread day after day.

The general method of control is to cover the leaf and stem with a protective layer of a fungicide so that when the spore drops on the surface of any part of the plant it will immediately be killed before it has a chance of sending down its roots into the tissue.

There are two main kinds of fungicide: the one based on sulphur, and the other on copper. In the case of sulphur, there is the ordinary 'flowers of sulphur', whose particles are rather too large and coarse to control fungus pests; there are sulphur dusts which are specially prepared, usually with a kaolin carrier, where the particles are very fine and can completely cover a leaf; there is the colloidal sulphur, which is very popular indeed, and rightly so; and the liver of sulphur spray, which perhaps is the most popular with private gardeners.

The disadvantage of using any sulphur preparations is that they do not mix happily with any of the white-oil or petroleum-oil preparations, and in fact, when sulphur in any form is used before or after any white-oil emulsion, scorching undoubtedly takes place. If it were not for this one could, in a general way, advise the use of colloidal sulphur for the mildews, and colloidal copper for the rusts. Actually, it probably pays to use colloidal copper only, for this can be mixed with a suitable white oil and gives excellent results also. Another advantage is that a colloidal copper wash does not leave an unpleasant stain on the leaves – it can be bought as Bouisol from most horticultural chemists and should be diluted in accordance with the instructions on the container. Some gardeners mix in nicotine as well, and even D.D.T. also, and say as a result that they have the all-in-one panacea for both fungus diseases and insect pests.

Leaf spot (Septoria chrysanthemi)

Dark brown patches appear on the upper surfaces of the leaves in the summer.

Control: Spray with a colloidal copper wash, using a suitable white oil as a spreader. Very severely attacked plants had better be burnt.

Mildew (Oidium chrysanthemi)

White powdery patches will be seen towards the end of the season, not only on the leaves, but on the stems as well. The white growth starts on the under surface, and in bad attacks the leaves will turn a brownish colour and will eventually drop off. It is a disease which may occur out of doors under conditions where the soil is dry, and therefore it always helps to keep chrysanthemums properly watered in dry weather.

Under glass, the disease is encouraged by damp, humid conditions, and it helps to have a little heat to provide a buoyant atmosphere.

Control: Spray with a colloidal copper wash from the end of May onwards if the trouble is seen. In bad years it may be necessary to spray once a fortnight until the flowers start to show.

If white oil is not going to be used at all, spray with a colloidal sulphur wash such as Sulsol with a suitable spreader.

Mould (Botrytis chrysanthemi)

If the plants are grown properly in the greenhouse they will never be attacked by the grey mould disease often known as Botrytis. It can easily be recognised by the greyish fluffy appearance on the undersides of the petals or on the dead stems or leaves. I have seen it give a good deal of trouble, even in the early stages, when plants are over-crowded, and especially in cold houses where the conditions are humid.

Control: There is no fungicide which will cure the trouble. The great thing to do is to ensure the free circulation of air, and this will be helped if a little heat can be put on, and the ventilators opened. Every good gardener knows that when grey mould is seen the atmosphere is not only too moist but cold as well.

Rust (*Puccinia chrysanthemi*)

This can be a very bad disease indeed, and particularly with certain varieties such as Gladys Paine and Mrs R. G. James. It seems to be particularly virulent in some years, and is undoubtedly carried over by spores dropping on to the young shoots as they appear above ground level before the old leaves are dead. Red rusty spots are usually seen first on the under surfaces of the leaves; these may be in ring formation. On the upper surfaces of the leaves light yellow circular dots appear which, of course, correspond to the rusty pustules found below. As the disease progresses, so the leaves turn brown, and in the case of Friendly Rival they may drop off.

The writer has discovered that plants that have been manured excessively with nitrogen are more easily attacked, and the trouble is far more extensive in wet seasons than in dry ones.

Control: Spray with Bouisol immediately the trouble is seen, and burn, if possible, the old stools and leaves which have been infected.

Virus

Though not a true disease, the chrysanthemum virus is included here, largely because it is not an insect pest. The main one which seems to be causing trouble is usually called the 'chrysanthemum mosaic', caused by a virus related to the Cucumber Virus 1 group. The leaves generally show some discoloration, and when the flowers open it is seen that there has been a breaking of the colour into, say, two or three different shades, as well as a certain amount of distortion. In the case of the reflexed varieties, the outer petals may stick up like quills, being rolled. In other cases the blooms will have a tousled appearance. There are, of course, mild symptoms and severe ones.

Control: It is probable that the virus is transmitted by aphides and, of course, it is carried over in cuttings; it is therefore important to burn badly infected plants in the autumn so that cuttings are never saved from them, as well as to spray regularly with nicotine to control the aphides.

PESTS

In all my books I am always glad to give credit where credit is due, and in my book, *The ABC of Pests and Diseases*, I thanked my old friend Mr G. Fox Wilson, as well as such experts as Dr H. W. Miles, Mr S. G. Jary, and others. Once again I have not hesitated to seek advice, and so I must thank the late G. Fox Wilson and others who have worked so hard to help the chrysanthemum growers. As at the present time we are growing some thousands of chrysanthemums at the Horticultural Training Centre, Thaxted, we have indeed much to be thankful for.

One can divide all insect pests into two big classes: those which suck, like the capsid bugs and the aphides; and those which nibble or eat, like the defoliating caterpillars. There are, of course, others which tunnel like the leaf miner; and the Frosted Orange Moth, which burrows into the stem. Unfortunately there are probably over eighty distinct species of insect pests which will attack chrysanthemums, and the grower therefore has to be on his guard. It is not proposed to include every single pest which may cause trouble, but merely the most important, or, in fact, those that are commonly met with in almost all gardens.

The first thing to do is to examine the plant carefully and note the condition. Start with the buds. If these have been damaged, then suspect the earwig. If they have gone blind, then make certain the trouble is due to capsids.

Pass on to the foliage and look for aphides underneath the leaves. These, of course, are suckers. If on the other

M

hand the leaves are blackened, then the trouble is eelworm; if they are eaten away, you will suspect one of the many caterpillars, the flea beetle, or the slug; if there are any signs of galls, then the trouble will be the chrysanthemum gall midge; and if the leaves are tunnelled and mined, you will know that it is the leaf miner. On the other hand, if the leaves are mottled, you will suspect the sucking leaf hopper, the red spider or the white fly; while if the foliage is puckered or scarred, it is that capsid bug again; while the sooty moulds indicate a mealy-bug attack.

Now examine the flowers. If they are discoloured, then it is sure to be thrips; if they are eaten away at all, suspect cockroaches, earwigs, crickets, or the caterpillars of the Angle Shades Moth. If, on the other hand, the blooms are malformed in any way, it is the capsid bug once more.

Follow carefully down the shoots and stems. If they are distorted, it is probably due to the Frog-hopper or Cuckoo-spit. If they are eaten away, it will be millipedes; if they are severed at ground level or above, the trouble has been the caterpillars of the Hart and Dart Moth or of one of the other moths like the Turnip or Yellow Underwing. The tunnelling in the lower stem may be wireworm, or in the upper part of the stem the grub of the Frosted Orange Moth.

Do not forget that the roots may be attacked also. There a root aphis, for example, which sucks. There are leather jackets, millipedes, vine weevils and caterpillars of the Garden Swift Moth which actually eat the roots, and there is the stool-mining maggot as well, while if galls are found on the roots then you know that the trouble is the Root-Knot Eelworm.

Aphides (green flies, black flies, etc.) (Aphis spp.)

Aphides breed quickly; they feed by sucking the sap. They curl the leaves, distort the shoots and cause malformed flowers. If they are not checked on the plants outside, they may easily be carried in on the leaves into the greenhouse, and then they will go on producing young or laying eggs throughout the winter months.

Control: Again and again throughout the book, I have suggested the spraying with nicotine using 1 ounce of pure liquid nicotine in 10 gallons of water, plus 3 ounces of a spreader like Shellestol. Some will prefer to use a proprietary nicotine insecticide such as Venetan. Routine fortnightly applications are most effective. The wash should be applied to the undersides of the leaves as well as to the tips of the shoots.

In the case of plants growing in the greenhouse, nicotine should be used for fumigation purposes, and special nicotine fumigative may be bought for the purpose.

Capsid Bugs (*Lygus pabulinus*, *Lygus pratensis*, *Lygus lucorum*)
These capsid bugs are given common names like the Tarnished Plant Bug, the Bishop Bug, the Potato Capsid, and so on. The worst trouble usually occurs from about the middle of July to the middle of October. Sometimes the capsids are brought into the greenhouses on to the plants late in September, and then they continue to give trouble during the winter months. Outside, the capsids may shelter among rubbish, in the cracks of fencing, and so on, and then become a nuisance again in the spring. They are suckers, and they push a needle-like proboscis into the leaves or buds, or even shoots, and thus they stunt, check growth, pucker leaves, and cause malformed blooms.

Control: It is most important to keep down weeds and thus to reduce alternative hosts. All debris that collects under hedgerows should be cleared up, and any currant or gooseberry bushes which may be growing in the garden must be sprayed with D.N.C. in the late winter to kill the eggs of this pest.

On the chrysanthemums themselves, spray with a good D.D.T. emulsion from early July until the middle of September, say once every three weeks. Give a good soaking, not only to the plants, but to the soil around, so that any capsids that drop to the ground may be killed also. A good D.D.T. spraying usually is effective for about three weeks.

Caterpillars

There are a number of different kinds of caterpillars which will eat the leaves, and some like those of the Angle Shades Moth will feed on the buds and the petals. Some caterpillars feed during the day and others during the night.

Control: Spray immediately the trouble is seen, with an efficient D.D.T. wash. The emulsion should contain 20 per cent D.D.T., and the usual formula is to dissolve one tablespoonful of such a concentrate in $1\frac{1}{2}$ gallons of water. Where water is a difficulty a 5 per cent D.D.T. dust may be used instead early in the morning, while the dew is still on the plants. Under glass D.D.T. smokes should be used. These are placed on the path in accordance with the instructions given on the packet, the ventilators are closed and the wicks or fuses are then lit. Shut the door carefully, and then open up early in the morning.

Chrysanthemum Midge (*Diarthronomyia chrysanthemi*)

This can be a very bad pest. The whitish larvæ feed right inside the tissue of the plants and produce thorn-shaped galls. The trouble is usually seen and first noticed on the leaves, but in bad cases the stems may be attacked, and also the buds; flowers may be badly distorted and the plants extremely stunted as a result. Chrysanthemums which are badly attacked throw few cuttings and it is a good plan to burn all stools of seriously infected plants.

Control: Fortnightly sprayings with nicotine help tremendously in controlling this pest, especially if any infected leaves can be picked off and burnt. I have known the trouble to start as a result of infected cuttings being received from a nursery. Some gardeners therefore suspect all bought in cuttings and put them, as it were, in quarantine for a fortnight or so.

Under glass D.D.T. smoke bombs are very effective, as are D.D.T. Aerosols.

Cockroaches (*Blatta orientalis and Periplaneta americana*)

These work at night time, and damage the flowers in a similar manner to the crickets. They also like heated houses.

Control: Dust with a good D.D.T. dust as for crickets (see below) and spray the flower buds with wettable D.D.T. if necessary.

Crickets (*Gryllus domesticus*)

Crickets work at night time, and usually feed on the petals of the flowers. Occasionally they may damage the leaves. The damage they do is often thought to be that of earwigs or caterpillars. They love living in heated houses and will often go from one greenhouse to another.

Control: Dust the floor with a 5 per cent D.D.T. dust and sprinkle this along the back of the hot-water pipes as well. It helps too if the flower buds are sprayed with wettable D.D.T.

Cuckoo-Spit (*sometimes called the Frog-Hopper*) (*Philaenus spumarius*)

Most people know the spittle-like appearance of this trouble. The pest surrounds itself with this excretion so as to prevent being eaten by birds. The insect, however, will produce a severe check to growth and may distort the shoots and stems.

Control: The moment the Cuckoo-Spit is seen, dust with a good nicotine dust. This gives the best results when the air temperature is 65 deg. F. Another alternative is to spray with a nicotine wash (formula: 1 ounce of nicotine, 2 ounces of a good spreader like Shellestol to 10 gallons of water).

Cutworms (*sometimes called Surface Caterpillars*) (*Agrotis exclamationis, Triphaena orbona, Triphaena pronuba*)

The caterpillars feed at night time and usually sever the stem just below soil level, but sometimes just above. They can do a lot of damage any time between the beginning of August and the end of October. During the day they hide just under the soil.

Control: The method of control is to use a bait consisting of ¼ lb. of Paris Green to 7 lb. of bran or breadcrumbs. Mix the ingredients together, add a little water to form a crumbly mash, and broadcast the bait evenly over the ground late in the evening, wherever the trouble is seen. The quantity given above should be sufficient for about 1/16th of an acre.

Earwigs (*Forficula auricularia*)

Some have said that earwigs never damage chrysanthemums, but this is not true. They are often found feeding on the open flowers, and they may attack the leaves as well. They do their work at night time, and they shelter during the day under stones, in the internodes of bamboo canes, and in cracks in between bricks. The damage is similar to that caused by crickets.

Control: See Crickets.

Eelworms (Aphelenchoides ritzema-bosi)

There are two main eelworms that attack chrysanthemums. The leaf eelworm and the root-knot eelworm. In the case of the latter, this pest will feed on almost any plant, and it causes the roots to become swollen and galled, and in bad cases the whole of the root system will be destroyed and ruined. The plants usually wilt soon after being watered. The only satisfactory method of control is to steam-sterilise the soil, or to apply a new compound known as D.D.

Control: In the case of the leaf eelworm, the control is to give the stools' warm-water treatment as described in Chapter IV, page 29. Another method which has given good results recently is to spray with Phosferno 20, the first in the rooted-cuttings stage and the second a month later. This is a Parathion mixture which must be used with care (formula: 1 fluid ounce Phosferno 20 in 5 gallons of water).

Flea Beetles (Longitaisus succineus)

Tiny little black beetles which suck the foliage and often eat out tiny portions between the leaf veins.

Control: Spray with a 30 per cent wettable D.D.T., or dust well with a 5 per cent D.D.T. dust.

Leaf Hoppers (Eupteryx auratus, Eupteryx melissae, Erythroneura pallidifrons)

These are similar to capsid bugs in the way they work. They cause bleached areas to appear on the leaves; on occasions the mottling is quite severe. During 'moulting' they cast their skins, and these will be found on the undersides of the leaves. Some people have mistaken these for the pest.

Control: Spray as advised for Capsids.

Leaf Miners (Phytomyza atricornis)

The leaves are mined or tunnelled tortuitously, some-times so badly that the foliage drops to the ground pre-maturely. In bad cases, of course, the growth is checked seriously. The female flies suck the leaves and may cause small bleached areas. Some gardeners have attributed this to damage by capsid bugs. The females lay their eggs in the leaves, and when these hatch out the little larvæ start to do their tunnelling. When they are fully grown they pupate in the leaf, and it should be possible to see the yellowy brown pupa sticking out slightly from one of the tunnels on the underside of a leaf.

Control: Spray with nicotine regularly, say once a fort-night, for re-infections may come from other plants, par-ticularly sow thistles. The use of a good Gammexane dust is also an excellent way of controlling this pest.

Leather Jackets (Tipula spp.)

These are the larvæ of the Daddy Long Legs, and in the North the grub is called the Bot. It is 1 to 1½ inches long when fully grown and of a greyish-brown or blackish colour. It is legless and has a dull leathery skin. The trouble usually starts early in September by these creatures nibbling the roots.

Control: Use the Paris Green and bran or breadcrumbs bait as advised for Cutworms on page 172.

Mealy Bugs (Pseudococcus spp.)

This is a pest that, as a rule, will only attack chrysanthe-mums in cases where plants are brought into the greenhouse infected with the trouble. The pests cause the leaves to look very dirty, while the bugs themselves appear to be covered with a little wool-like substance – hence the term 'meal'.

The control is to spray with nicotine (usual formula), or

to use the new H.E.T.P. Three thorough soakings must be given at 5-day intervals.

Red Spider (*Tetranychus telarius*)

These little mites, which are not really red and do not look like spiders to the uninitiated, are found on the under surfaces of the leaves, where they suck the sap and cause mottled and bleached areas. Pinkish eggs may be laid under the leaves among silken threads. These can be seen with a magnifying glass. In the autumn the mites over-winter in the brickwork of the greenhouses, in cracks in the wood-work, in bamboo canes, and so on.

Control: Good control can be effected by the use of Azobenzene in a smoke bomb, or Aerosol.

Stem Tunnelling Caterpillar (*Frosted Orange Moth*) (*Gortyna flavago*)

If the foliage is seen to wilt, look down to the lower part of the stem to see whether there is a hole out of which an excretion is coming. This is sometimes called 'frass'.

Once the caterpillar has tunnelled well up the stem, there is nothing that can be done other than to cut off the infected portion and burn it.

Control: In gardens where it is discovered that this pest is increasing Gammexane should be dusted all round the stems of the plants once a fortnight, from early August until the end of September. This will discourage the egg-laying female. Keep the land clean by hoeing, because the alternative host plants of this pest are thistles, docks, burdock and agrimony.

Stool Miner (*Psila nigricornis*)

A fly appears in April or May, and eggs are laid on the soil near the plant. The yellowy white larvæ, like wireworms, feed on the roots and tunnel into the underground stems. Deep wounds will appear because the tissues will split. Much damage to the stools is done during the autumn.

Control: Dust with Gammexane to keep away the egg-laying females, and when an attack has been seen water the ground around the stools with a corrosive sublimate solution (formula: $\frac{1}{4}$ ounce mercuric chloride to $2\frac{1}{2}$-gallon can of water).

Slugs (*Agriolimax reticulatus*)

Most people know this pest, though some gardeners do not realise that there is a kind which is very small indeed and yet can do a lot of damage.

Control: Mix powdered metaldehyde with powdered breadcrumbs; one metaldehyde bar crushed is enough for a tumblerful of crumbs. Put down small heaps of the bait about the size of an eggcup, 2 or 3 feet apart all over the area concerned. Repeat the dose again if necessary a fortnight later.

Thrips (*Thrips flavus, Thrips fuscipennis, Thrips nigropilosus, and Thrips tabaci*)

These tiny little black insects which can hardly be seen with the naked eye are not only minute but narrow bodied as well. They are usually discovered by tapping a plant over a clean white handkerchief and noticing if little black specks drop on to it. Some of the wingless nymphs are almost colourless. These creatures puncture and bruise the leaf tissues with their mouths, and they are partly suckers. They do their feeding on the undersides of the leaves, and a silver mottling is seen on the upper surface of the foliage.

Later they will get into the flower buds and flowers. They cause the petals to be streaked and discoloured, and they may be the means of the outer petals shrivelling altogether.

The quality of blooms may be completely spoiled. It is a particularly bad pest in a dry season.

Control: D.D.T. gives excellent control. Out of doors it is possible to spray with a D.D.T. emulsion or to dust with a 5 per cent D.D.T. dust. In the greenhouse one of the D.D.T. aerosols may be used, or a D.D.T. smoke bomb. When sprays are applied they must be put on with such force so that the insects on the undersides of the leaves are actually hit. It always pays to syringe chrysanthemums in hot dry weather, as this helps to control this pest.

White Fly (*Trialeurodes vaporariorum*)

Most people know the white fly which attacks all kinds of greenhouse plants. When the plants are touched the flies may rise like a cloud. The nymphs are scale-like and are attached to the undersides of the leaves. They give out a certain amount of honeydew, with the result that a sooty-mould type of fungus may live on this substance and cause the underside of the foliage to look black.

Control: There is a parasite known as the Chalcid Wasp (*Encarsia formosa*) which may be introduced into the house and which will in consequence keep down the pest in nature's way. The R.H.S. usually have a supply of this parasite available to members. The other alternative is to fumigate with hydrogen cyanide, a dust which can be purchased from the horticultural chemist for this purpose if the 'poison book' is signed. D.D.T. smoke bombs also give good results, as do D.D.T. aerosols.

Wireworms (*Agriotes spp.*)

Most people know wireworms, which are the larvæ of the click beetle. This beetle may be seen flying about in the sun during the months of May and June, and the larvæ which hatch out in a month's time feed on the roots of grass as a rule. They go on growing and usually remain in the soil for four or five years before turning into beetles again. They may be distinguished from millepedes and centipedes by the number of legs. Wireworms have only three pairs of short legs, situated on the first three segments of their bodies. Millepedes and centipedes have legs all down their bodies. Wireworms are, as their name suggests, very wiry and difficult to kill by squeezing between the fingers.

They attack the roots of chrysanthemums and the underground stems, and I have known them to tunnel up the stems for 6 inches or more. In the greenhouse they can be a nuisance, because they are usually introduced in the loam.

Control: It is important, therefore, to sterilise loam either by steam or by fumigating with carbon bi-sulphide. In the open, excellent control can be achieved by using the non-tainting Gammexane, which should be applied at the rate of 2 ounces to the square yard and be well raked in.

INDEX

A

Alpha-naphthalene acetic acid, 39
Anemone-centred Chrysanthemums, 147
   stopping of, 65
Aphides, 31, 32, 33, 34, 75, 84, 88, 102, 170
Axil of leaf, 19, 35
Azobenzene, 177

B

Basal cuttings, 35
   growths, 20, 95
B.D.H. Soil Indicator, 45, 69, 70
Beta-indolylacetic acid, 39
Botrytis, 167
Bouisol, 82, 166, 168
Brosson sprinkler, 76
Bud, terminal, 23
Buds, securing of, 22, 53, 63

C

Capsid bugs, 75, 84, 171
Carbon bi-sulphide, 180
Cascade chrysanthemums, 149
Caterpillars, 84, 172
   stem-tunnelling, 177
   surface, 177
Chalcid wasp, 179
Charm chrysanthemums, 155
Cheshire School of Agriculture, 54
Chrysanthemum, early, *see under* Earlies
Chrysanthemum maximum, 104
Chrysanthemum midge, 172
Chrysanthemum Rubellum, 162
Chrysanthemums
   in pots, 85
      feeding, 93
      housing, 96
      potting, 86
      potting on, 87, 89
      staking, 91
      standing ground for, 90
      stopping, 89, 92
      varieties, 98
      ventilation of, 87, 97
      watering, 89, 93

Chrysanthemums—*cont.*
   lifted in, 81
      feeding, 83
      varieties, 84
      watering, 83
   single-flowering, 104
      early, 105
      exhibiting of, 115
      late, 105
Cloches, 43, 72
Cockroaches, 173
Compost (*see also under* John Innes Compost), 19
   requirements of, 44
Counting down, 25
Crickets, 173
Crown buds, 21
Crowns, third, 26
Cuckoo spit, 173
Cuprinol, 80
Cuttings, 18, 34
   basal, 35
   compost for, 36
   correct kinds of, 34
   feeding; 40, 51
   heated frames for, 38
   hormones for, 39
   in pots, 42
   insertion of, 36
   moving of, 39
   stem, 35
   striking, 19, 36
   ventilation of, 37, 40
   watering, 38, 40
Cutworms, 174

D

Daddy long legs, 176
D.D., 175
D.D.T., 166, 172, 173, 175, 179
Decoratives, stopping of, 65
'Dedutchable house', 78, 81
Disbudding, 76
Disc floret, 24
D.N.C., 172
Drivall, 80